# CALL to FAITH

## GRADE 4
*Parish*

# Harcourt Religion Publishers

www.harcourtreligion.com

**Nihil Obstat**
Rev. Dennis J. Colter

**Imprimatur**
☩ Most Rev. Jerome Hanus, OSB
Archbishop of Dubuque
January 5, 2004
Feast of Saint John Neumann

The Ad Hoc Committee to Oversee the Use of the Catechism, United States Conference of Catholic Bishops, has found this catechetical text, © 2005, to be in conformity with the *Catechism of the Catholic Church.*

The Imprimatur is an official declaration that a book or pamphlet is free of doctrinal or moral error. No implication is contained therein that anyone who granted the Imprimatur agrees with the contents, opinions, or statements expressed.

For permission to reprint copyrighted material, grateful acknowledgment is made to the following sources:

*Confraternity of Christian Doctrine, Inc., Washington, D.C.:* Scriptures from the *New American Bible.* Text copyright © 1991, 1986, 1970 by Confraternity of Christian Doctrine, Inc. All rights reserved. No part of the *New American Bible* may be used or reproduced in any form, without permission in writing from the copyright owner.

*International Commission on English in the Liturgy:* English translation of "Come, Holy Spirit" (Retitled: "Prayer to the Holy Spirit") and "Memorare" from *A Book of Prayers.* Translation © 1982 by International Committee on English in the Liturgy, Inc. English translation of "Confiteor" ("I Confess"), "This is the Wood" (Retitled: "Honor the Cross") and "Holy is God" in *The Roman Missal.* Translation © 1973 by International Committee on English in the Liturgy, Inc.

*International Consultation on English Texts:* English translation of Glory to the Father, The Lord's Prayer, Hail Mary and *Kyrie Eleison* by the International Consultation on English Texts (ICET).

Additional acknowledgments appear on page 248.

Printed in the United States of America

0-15-901220-1

5 6 7 8 9 10   030   10 09 08 07

# Grade 4 Contents

© Harcourt Religion

v

# Catholic Source Book

# About You

**Let Us Pray**

**Leader:** Loving God, help us to learn your way.
"Blessed are you, O Lord;
    teach me your laws."

*Psalm 119:12*

**All:** Loving God, help us to learn your way.

**Activity** Let's Begin

**Looking Ahead** Welcome to the fourth grade. You have a whole new year of experiences ahead of you. You will have a new teacher, new classes, and possibly even new friends. You will learn more about your faith and about your life as a child of God.

You are special. What is the best thing about being you?

## What are some of your Favorite Things?

**Time of Day**

**Holiday**

**Book**

# About Your Faith

You are about to begin the next mile of your faith journey, but you do not travel alone. Your family, friends, and the whole parish community travel with you. This year you will read Bible stories and learn more about being a part of the Catholic Church.

## Activity

## Share Your Faith

**Reflect:** Think about something you already know about being Catholic.

**Share:** Share with a partner how you learned this.

**Act:** Write down one thing you know about being Catholic.

_____

_____

_____

_____

_____

_____

# About Your Book

Your book will help you to learn more about your faith, important people of faith, and ways Catholics celebrate faith.

Connect Your Faith

**Go On A Scavenger Hunt** As you read your book, you will find lots of different things. To get to know your book, look for the features listed below. Write down where you find each of them.

✝ SCRIPTURE                         Page _____

BIOGRAPHY                        Page _____

Words of Faith                   Page _____

Faith Fact                       Page _____

**People of Faith**      Page _____

 Let Us Pray                Page _____

 Focus                      Page _____

© Harcourt Religion

3

# A Call to Faith

## Gather

*Pray the Sign of the Cross together.*

Leader: Blessed be God.

All: **Blessed be God for ever.**

Leader: Let us pray.
*Bow your heads as the leader prays.*

All: **Amen.**

## Listen to God's Word

Reader: A reading from the holy Gospel according to Matthew.
*Read Matthew 9:9–13.*
The Gospel of the Lord.

All: **Praise to you, Lord Jesus Christ.**

## Dialogue

Why do you think Jesus went and ate with Matthew after he called him to be a disciple?

How can you answer Jesus' call to follow him?

## Prayer of the Faithful

Leader: Lord, the first disciples answered your call. They believed in you and followed you. We believe in you, too. Please hear our prayers.
*Respond to each prayer with these words.*

All: **Lord, hear our prayer.**

4

## Answer the Call

**Leader:** Matthew responded to Jesus' call to follow him. He welcomed Jesus into his life and his home. You can welcome Jesus into your life, too.

*Come forward as your name is called. Bow to the cross and say aloud "I will follow you, Jesus."*

You are all followers of Jesus. Welcome one another with a sign of his peace.

# Go Forth!

**Leader:** Let us go forth to welcome Christ into our lives.

**All:** **Thanks be to God.**

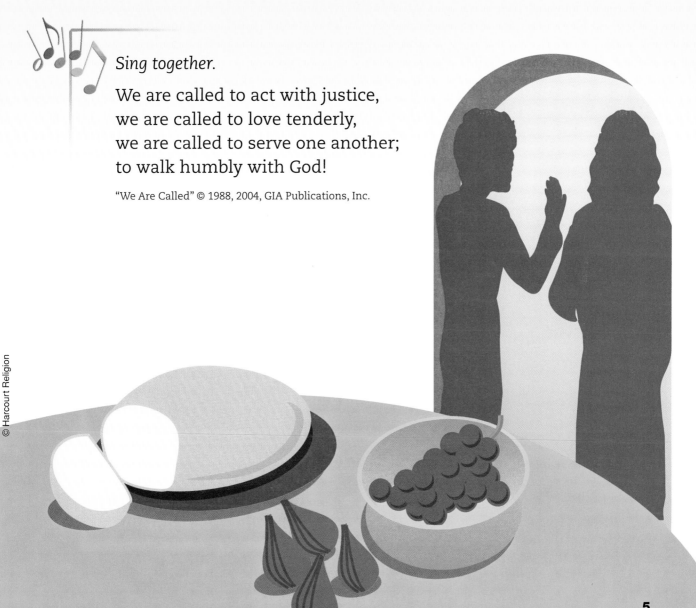

*Sing together.*

We are called to act with justice,
we are called to love tenderly,
we are called to serve one another;
to walk humbly with God!

"We Are Called" © 1988, 2004, GIA Publications, Inc.

# The Church's Seasons

**D**ifferent things happen at different times during the year. During fall, school starts and the leaves change color. In winter trees are bare and the days are short. When spring comes the flowers bloom, the days get longer, and people want to spend time outside. Summer brings warmer days, school break, and long hours of fun.

The Church has seasons, too. The seasons of the Church year recall important events in the lives of Jesus, Mary, and the saints. In every season the Church prays together to remember all the gifts that come from God the Father and his Son, Jesus.

The Church prays using different words and actions. Here are some of them.

## Words and Actions

The Bible is honored by bowing and sitting before it in silence.

The Cross is honored by kneeling in front of it or kissing it.

The sign of Christ's peace is offered with a handshake.

The Sign of the Cross is marked on foreheads, hearts, and lips.

Holy water is used as a reminder of Baptism.

Your class will use these words and actions to celebrate the different seasons.

# The Church Year

Advent

Christmas

Ordinary
Time

Ordinary
Time

Lent

Easter

Triduum

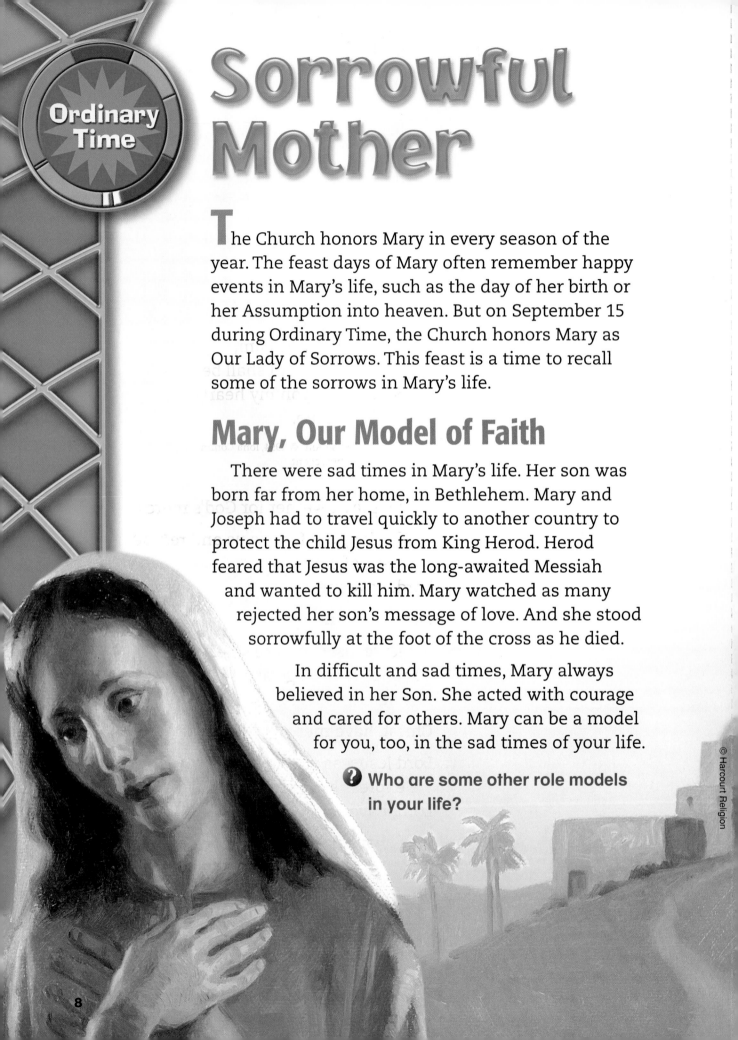

# Sorrowful Mother

**T**he Church honors Mary in every season of the year. The feast days of Mary often remember happy events in Mary's life, such as the day of her birth or her Assumption into heaven. But on September 15 during Ordinary Time, the Church honors Mary as Our Lady of Sorrows. This feast is a time to recall some of the sorrows in Mary's life.

## Mary, Our Model of Faith

There were sad times in Mary's life. Her son was born far from her home, in Bethlehem. Mary and Joseph had to travel quickly to another country to protect the child Jesus from King Herod. Herod feared that Jesus was the long-awaited Messiah and wanted to kill him. Mary watched as many rejected her son's message of love. And she stood sorrowfully at the foot of the cross as he died.

In difficult and sad times, Mary always believed in her Son. She acted with courage and cared for others. Mary can be a model for you, too, in the sad times of your life.

**?** Who are some other role models in your life?

# Celebrate Mary

## Gather

*Pray the Sign of the Cross together.*

Leader: Blessed be God.

All: **Blessed be God forever.**

*Sing together.*

Take, O take me as I am;
summon out what I shall be;
Set your seal upon my heart
    and live in me.

"Take, O Take Me As I Am" © 1994, Iona Community,
GIA Publications, Inc., agent

Leader: Let us pray together for God's mercy.

Lord Jesus, you forgive us and rescue us from
the pain of sin.
Lord, have mercy.

All: **Lord, have mercy.**

Leader: Christ Jesus, you have given us Mary as
a model of courage and patience.
Christ, have mercy.

All: **Christ, have mercy.**

Leader: Lord Jesus, as we remember Mary's sorrows,
we express sorrow for our failure to love.
Lord, have mercy.

All: **Lord, have mercy.**

Leader: Let us pray.

*Bow your heads as the leader prays.*

All: **Amen.**

# Listen to God's Word

Reader: A reading from the holy Gospel according to Luke.

*Read Luke 22:2–35.*
The Gospel of the Lord.

All: **Praise to you, Lord Jesus Christ.**

# Dialogue

Why did Simeon's message cause Mary sorrow?

If you had been in the Temple, what question would you have asked Simeon?

## Meditation

*Sit in silence before the cross as the leader leads you in a meditation on Our Lady of Sorrows.*

Leader: Let us pray . . .

All: **Amen.**

# Go Forth!

Leader: Let us go forth in Mary's spirit of faith, hope, and love for her Son.

All: **Thanks be to God.**

*Sing together.*

Take, O take me as I am;
summon out what I shall be;
set your seal upon my heart
  and live in me.

"Take, O Take Me As I Am" © 1994, Iona Community, GIA Publications, Inc.

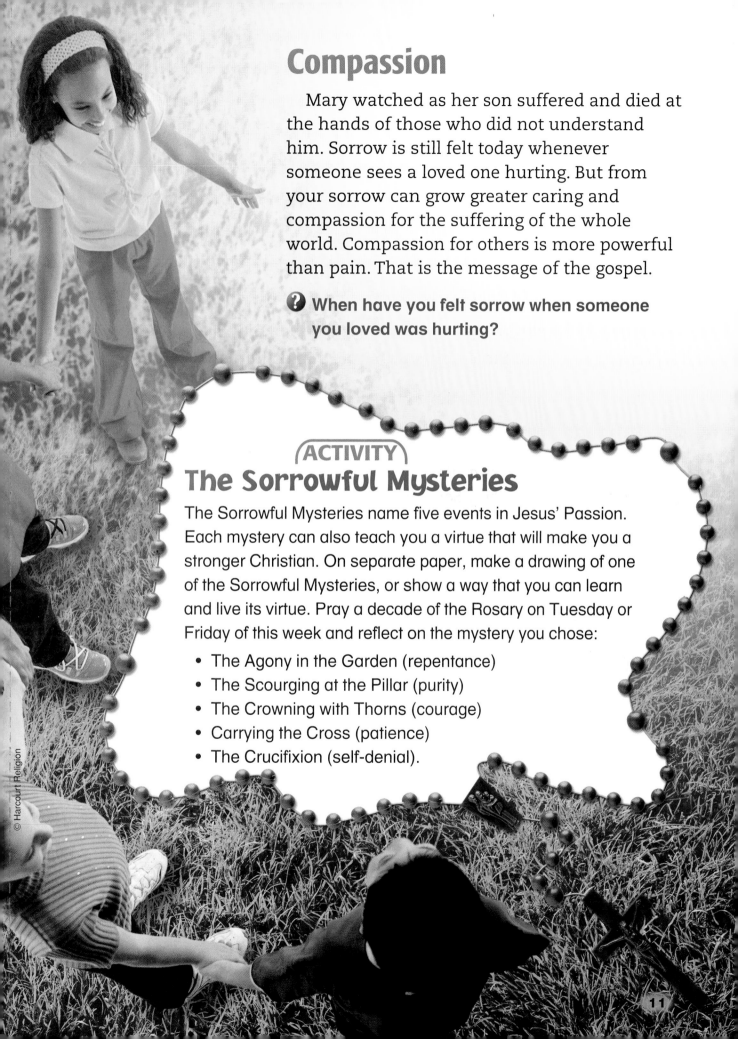

# Compassion

Mary watched as her son suffered and died at the hands of those who did not understand him. Sorrow is still felt today whenever someone sees a loved one hurting. But from your sorrow can grow greater caring and compassion for the suffering of the whole world. Compassion for others is more powerful than pain. That is the message of the gospel.

❷ **When have you felt sorrow when someone you loved was hurting?**

(ACTIVITY)

## The Sorrowful Mysteries

The Sorrowful Mysteries name five events in Jesus' Passion. Each mystery can also teach you a virtue that will make you a stronger Christian. On separate paper, make a drawing of one of the Sorrowful Mysteries, or show a way that you can learn and live its virtue. Pray a decade of the Rosary on Tuesday or Friday of this week and reflect on the mystery you chose:

- The Agony in the Garden (repentance)
- The Scourging at the Pillar (purity)
- The Crowning with Thorns (courage)
- Carrying the Cross (patience)
- The Crucifixion (self-denial).

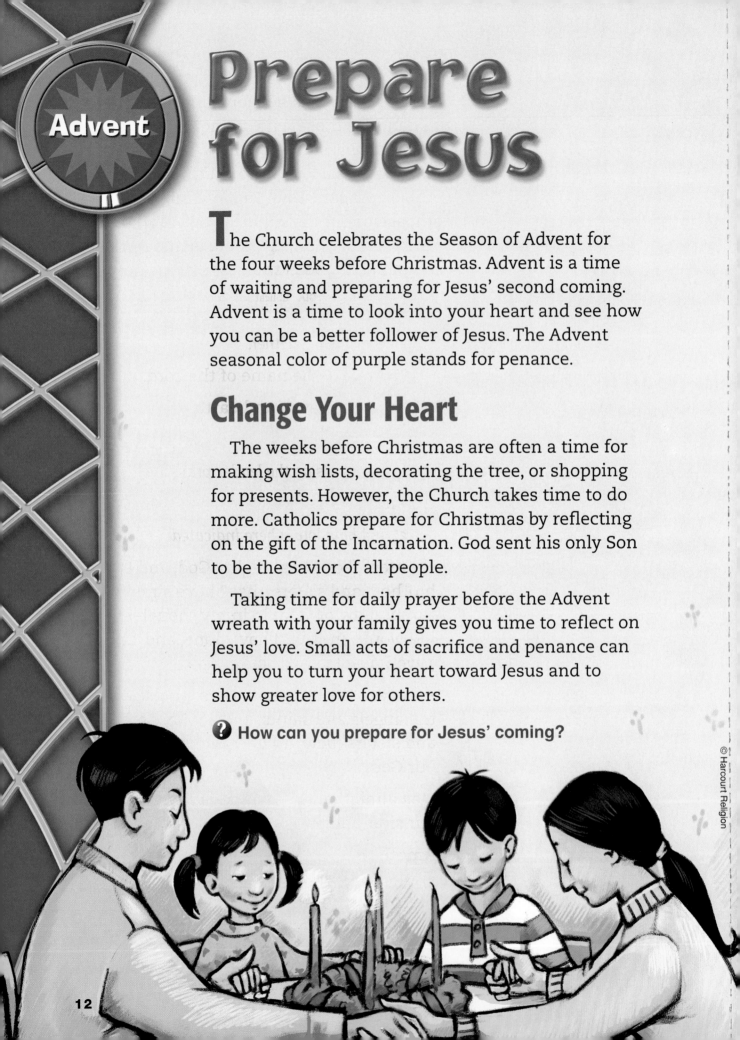

## Advent

# Prepare for Jesus

The Church celebrates the Season of Advent for the four weeks before Christmas. Advent is a time of waiting and preparing for Jesus' second coming. Advent is a time to look into your heart and see how you can be a better follower of Jesus. The Advent seasonal color of purple stands for penance.

## Change Your Heart

The weeks before Christmas are often a time for making wish lists, decorating the tree, or shopping for presents. However, the Church takes time to do more. Catholics prepare for Christmas by reflecting on the gift of the Incarnation. God sent his only Son to be the Savior of all people.

Taking time for daily prayer before the Advent wreath with your family gives you time to reflect on Jesus' love. Small acts of sacrifice and penance can help you to turn your heart toward Jesus and to show greater love for others.

**❓ How can you prepare for Jesus' coming?**

# Celebrate Advent

## Gather

*Sing together the refrain.*

Come, O Lord, change our hearts!
Emmanuel, God is with us.

"Come, O Lord" © 1997, GIA Publications, Inc.

*Pray the Sign of the Cross together.*

**Leader:** Our help is in the name of the Lord.

**All:** **Who made heaven and earth.**

**Leader:** Let us pray.

*Bow your heads as the leader prays.*

**All:** **Amen.**

*Kneel and bow low where indicated.*

I confess (bow) to almighty God, and to you, my brothers and sisters, that I have sinned (bow) through my own fault, in my thoughts and in my words, in what I have done, and in what I have failed to do;

And I ask the blessed Mary, ever virgin, all the angels and saints, and you, my brothers and sisters (bow), to pray for me to the Lord our God.

**Leader:** May almighty God have mercy on us, forgive us our sins, and bring us to everlasting life.

**All:** **Amen.**

# Listen to God's Word

Reader: A reading from the holy Gospel according to Mark.

Read Mark 1:1–8.
The Gospel of the Lord.

All: **Praise to you, Lord Jesus Christ.**

# Dialogue

How did John tell the people to prepare for the coming of the Messiah?

What does it mean to repent?

## Raise Hands in Prayer

*Sit before the wreath in silence and reflect on ways you will try to change your heart.*

Leader: Lord, we want your Spirit to change our hearts and prepare for your coming. Be with us as we pray.

*Stand, raise your hands, and pray the Lord's Prayer.*

Leader: Let us offer one another a greeting of peace as a sign of our desire to change our hearts.

*All exchange a sign of peace.*

# Go Forth!

Leader: Let us go forth to prepare the way of the Lord.

All: **Thanks be to God.**

14

# The Path of Love

John told the people who were waiting for the Messiah that they would have to change. He said, "Prepare the way of the Lord, make straight his paths" (*Mark 1:3*).

❓ **What changes can you make that will straighten your path and bring you closer to Jesus?**

## ACTIVITY
## Show Your Love

Make a coupon book of loving actions you can do for members of your family. You might include things like reading a book to a younger sibling, washing the dog without complaining, cleaning up your room, or taking someone's turn doing the dishes. Give one person in your family a coupon each day this week.

# God's Greatest Gift

The Church's Season of Christmas begins with the Mass of Christmas Eve on December 24 and continues for almost three weeks. The feast of Epiphany comes in the middle of the Christmas season. The season ends in January with the feast of the Baptism of the Lord, the Sunday after Epiphany.

The word *Epiphany* means "showing forth." On Epiphany the Church remembers the visit of the three magi, often called wise men, to the infant Jesus.

The magi came from distant lands, followed a bright star to find the infant Jesus, honored him, and gave glory to God. Epiphany celebrates the belief that Jesus came to earth to save everyone.

## Precious Gifts

To honor the Savior and show him reverence, the magi brought him gifts of gold, frankincense, and myrrh. The gift of gold, a precious metal, showed that they thought of Jesus as worthy of the highest honor. Frankincense, an incense with a pleasing smell, represented the holiness of Jesus. Myrrh is a symbol of preserving and saving. This gift was a sign that Jesus would die for the salvation of all people.

❓ **What gifts of reverence and worship can you offer Jesus?**

© Harcourt Religion

## Gather

*Pray the Sign of the Cross together.*

Leader: Blessed be the name of the Lord.

All: **Now and forever.**

*Sing together the refrain.*

O star of wonder, star of night,
Star with royal beauty bright,
Westward leading, still proceeding,
Guide us to the perfect Light.

"We Three Kings of Orient Are" Traditional

Leader: Let us pray.

*Bow your heads as the leader prays.*

All: **Amen.**

## Listen to God's Word

Reader: A reading from the holy gospel according to Matthew.

*Read Matthew 2:9–11.*
The Gospel of the Lord.

All: **Praise to you, Lord Jesus Christ.**

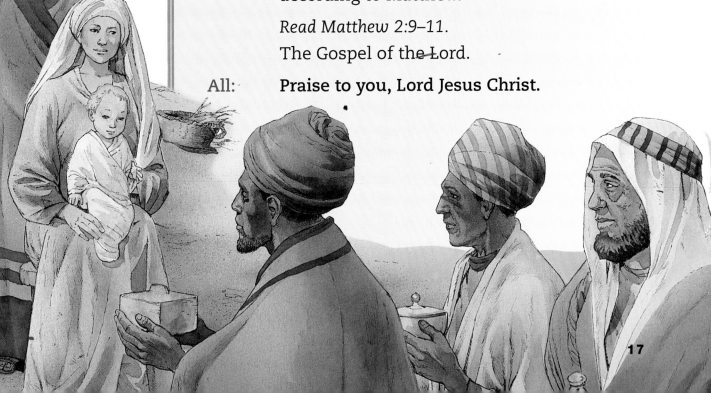

# Dialogue

Why did the magi honor the child Jesus?

How do you honor Jesus today?

## Procession of Gifts

Leader: May all kings bow before him,
all nations serve him.

*Psalm 72:11*

All: **Every nation will adore you.**

*Sing as you walk in procession, carrying the statues of the three kings. Place the statues and your Christmas promises in the crèche.*

# Go Forth!

Leader: Let us go forth to bring the Christmas gifts of peace, love, and joy to all we meet.

All: **Thanks be to God.**

*Sing together the refrain.*

O star of wonder, star of night,
Star with royal beauty bright,
Westward leading, still proceeding,
Guide us to the perfect Light.

"We Three Kings of Orient Are" Traditional

# Gifts from Jesus

The star led the magi to Jesus. They worshiped Jesus, the light of the world, bringing him gifts for a king. The gifts given to Jesus, he gives to you. By becoming one of us, Jesus brought all people the opportunity to be saved (myrrh), to be holy (frankincense), and to be honored (gold).

❓ In what ways have you seen Jesus' gifts of salvation, holiness, and dignity at work in the world?

## (ACTIVITY)
## Make a Group Mural

Make a group mural entitled, "Gifts for All." Draw a way that you will bring the message of Jesus to others in the weeks ahead.

# Called to Leadership

The Church celebrates the feasts of many saints during Ordinary Time. The feast of the conversion of Saint Paul highlights an important event in his life and in the life of the Church. The Church celebrates Saint Paul's conversion on January 25.

## A Change of Heart

Paul was born a Jew in Jesus' time. His Jewish name was Saul. Paul was a faithful Jew, and he worried as he watched the growth in numbers of Jesus' followers after Jesus' death. He saw these disciples as a threat to his traditional Jewish beliefs. Paul began bringing them to the authorities in order to arrest them.

Everything changed when Paul met Jesus on the road to Damascus. He was traveling there to punish some Christians. Instead he experienced the Risen Christ in a vision. Jesus said to him, "Saul, Saul, why are you persecuting me?" (Acts 22:7). After that Paul changed his ways.

Paul became a central figure in the growth of the early Church. Because he met the Risen Christ as the Apostles did, he is called an Apostle, too. His missionary journeys, his many letters, and the power of his preaching helped Christianity to spread far and wide in the world.

❷ **What are some ways your parish preaches the good news?**

# Celebrate Paul

## Gather

*Pray the Sign of the Cross together.*

**Leader:** Our help is in the name of the Lord.

**All:** **Who made heaven and earth.**

*Sing together the refrain.*

All grownups, all children,
   all mothers, all fathers
Are sisters and brothers in the fam'ly of God.

"All Grownups, All Children" © 1997, GIA Publications, Inc.

**Leader:** Let us pray.

*Bow your heads as the leader prays.*

**All:** **Amen.**

## Listen to God's Word

**Reader:** A reading from the Acts of the Apostles.

*Read Acts 9:19–22.*
The word of the Lord.

**All:** **Thanks be to God.**

## Dialogue

How did Paul change as a result of meeting the Risen Christ?

What gifts did Saint Paul bring to the Church?

## Signing of the Senses

*Step forward one by one as the leader signs your eyes, lips, and hands with the cross of salvation. After each person is signed, say the following.*

**All:**     **Christ will be your strength!**
             **Learn to know and follow him!**

GIA Publications

*After the signing of the senses, bow your head as the leader prays.*

**Leader:** Lord Jesus, we place ourselves entirely under the sign of your cross, in the name of the Father, and of the Son, and of the Holy Spirit.

**All:**     **Amen.**

# Go Forth!

**Leader:** Let us go forth in the spirit of Saint Paul to bring the message of Jesus to all.

**All:**     **Thanks be to God.**

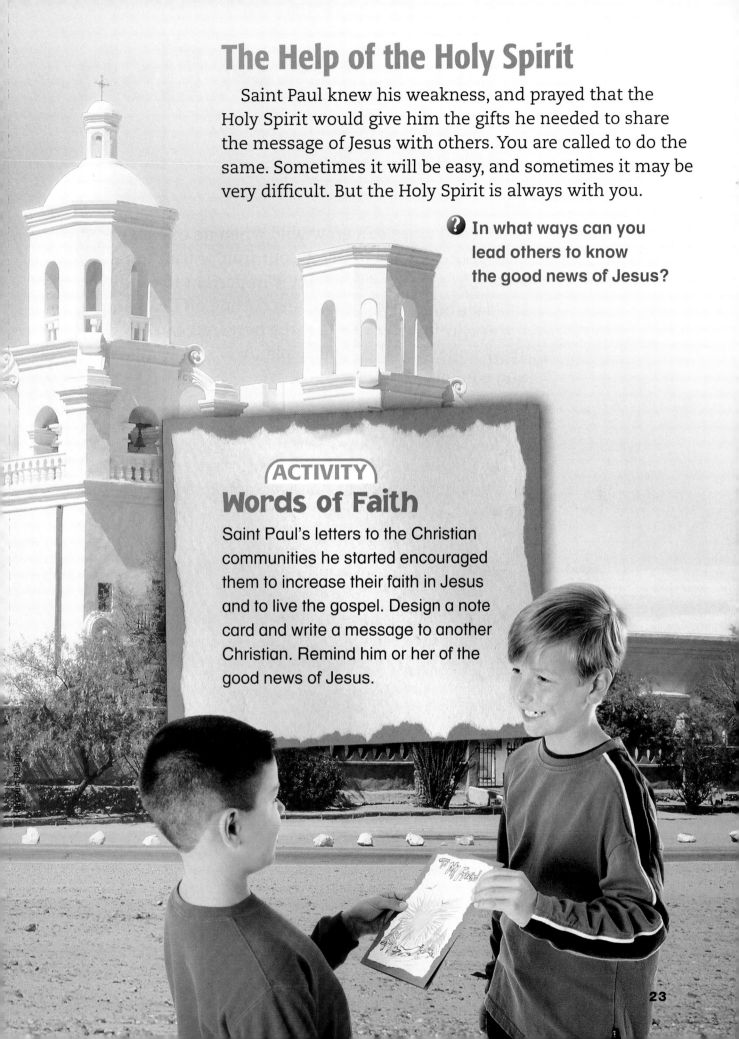

# The Help of the Holy Spirit

Saint Paul knew his weakness, and prayed that the Holy Spirit would give him the gifts he needed to share the message of Jesus with others. You are called to do the same. Sometimes it will be easy, and sometimes it may be very difficult. But the Holy Spirit is always with you.

❓ In what ways can you lead others to know the good news of Jesus?

## ACTIVITY
## Words of Faith

Saint Paul's letters to the Christian communities he started encouraged them to increase their faith in Jesus and to live the gospel. Design a note card and write a message to another Christian. Remind him or her of the good news of Jesus.

# An Unselfish Spirit

Trees and vines can grow wild when no one takes care of them. They produce sour fruit or fruit too small to enjoy. That is why it is important to prune trees and vines. *Pruning* means cutting off dead and unhealthy branches so that the best fruit can grow. Trees and vines also require plenty of soil, water, and sunlight.

## Spiritual Discipline

During the Season of Lent, the Church reminds you that good pruning is needed to produce good fruit. As a follower of Jesus, you can produce good fruit by cutting away bad habits and selfishness. Then the good fruit of love, sharing, and forgiveness can grow in you.

Prayer, fasting, and almsgiving are the three principal practices of Lent. These are the practices of disciples of Jesus. Prayer is the foundation for all spiritual discipline. It is like the soil a tree needs to grow. It gives you spiritual nourishment and deepens your relationship with God.

❓ **What are some things you can prune away to grow as a follower of Jesus?**

# Celebrate Lent

## Gather

*Sing together.*

O Lord, hear my prayer,
    O Lord, hear my prayer:
when I call answer me.
O Lord, hear my prayer,
    O Lord, hear my prayer,
Come and listen to me.

"O Lord, Hear My Prayer" © 1982, Les Presses de Taizé,
GIA Publications, Inc., agent

*Pray the Sign of the Cross together.*

**Leader:** Oh Lord, open my lips.

**All:** **That my mouth shall proclaim your praise.**

**Leader:** Let us pray.

*Raise your hands as the leader prays.*

**All:** **Amen.**

## Listen to God's Word

**Reader:** A reading from the holy Gospel according
to Matthew.

*Read Matthew 6:5–8.*
The Gospel of the Lord.

**All:** **Praise to you, Lord Jesus Christ.**

## Dialogue

Why does Jesus say that it is better to pray in secret?

How can prayer help you to yield "good fruit"?

### Kneel in Silence

*Quietly ask God to strengthen you to turn toward his love and to be faithful to the gospel.*

## Intercessions

Leader: God does not desire our death but rather that we should turn from our sins and have life. Let us pray that we may sin no more and so bear good fruit.

*Respond to each intercession with these words.*

All: **Lord, hear our prayer.**

# Go Forth!

Leader: Lord, may our Lenten prayer strengthen us so that we may bear good fruit and be good news.

All: **Thanks be to God.**

# Growing Spiritually

Your body is growing every day. Growing in spirit is equally important. Just as you feed your body, so must your soul be fed. The spiritual discipline of prayer strengthens you so that you can avoid sin and prepare for the joy of Easter.

❓ **What habits of prayer do you already have?**

❓ **What is your plan for strengthening your life of prayer during this Lent?**

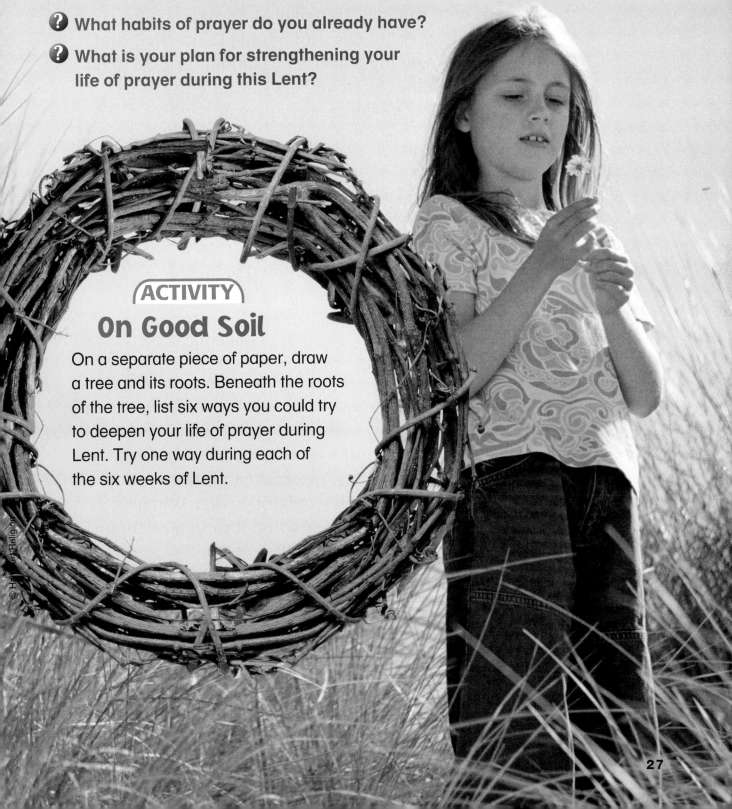

## ( ACTIVITY )

### On Good Soil

On a separate piece of paper, draw a tree and its roots. Beneath the roots of the tree, list six ways you could try to deepen your life of prayer during Lent. Try one way during each of the six weeks of Lent.

# The Suffering Servant

The Triduum is the holiest of all celebrations. It starts with the Holy Thursday Mass, moves into Good Friday, continues through the Easter Vigil, and ends with evening prayer on Easter Sunday. On Good Friday the Church remembers the suffering Jesus endured for the sake of every person.

## The Cross

Jesus' journey carrying his cross from the place he was condemned to the place where he was crucified is called the Way of the Cross. It was a time of physical and emotional pain. The Romans used the crucifixion as an instrument of punishment and death. Yet through Jesus the cross became a sign of new life.

Because of Jesus' death on the cross and his Resurrection to new life, you receive forgiveness and share in God's life.

Today, the cross is a symbol of Jesus' love for all. The cross can inspire you to love in both word and action. Whenever you spread peace and love, you celebrate Jesus' victory on the cross.

❓ **Where do you see crosses?**

# Celebrate Triduum

## Gather

*Pray the Sign of the Cross together.*

Leader: O Lord, open my lips.

All: **That my mouth may proclaim your praise.**

*Sing together.*

O how good is Christ the Lord!
On the cross he died for me.
In three days he rose again. Glory be to Jesus!
Glory be to Jesus! Glory be to Jesus!
In three days he rose again. Glory be to Jesus!

"O How Good Is Christ the Lord" Puerto Rican traditional

Leader: Let us pray.

*Bow your heads as the leader prays.*

All: **Amen.**

## Listen to God's Word

Reader: A reading from the Book of the prophet Isaiah.

*Read Isaiah 53:10–12.*

The word of the Lord.

All: **Thanks be to God**

## Dialogue

The Book of Isaiah was written long before the birth of Jesus. Why do you think the Church reads this passage on Good Friday?

## Intercessions

*After each intercession, kneel for a moment in silent prayer, then stand as the leader prays.*

### Honor the Cross

**Leader:** This is the wood of the cross, on which hung the Savior of the world.

**All:** Come. Let us worship.

*Stand and say the following acclamation three times, bowing deeply first to the left, then to the right, then to the center, always facing the cross.*

**All:** Holy is God!
Holy and Strong!

*Step forward in silence, one by one, and reverence the cross by bowing, kissing the cross, or offering some other sign of reverence.*

## Go Forth!

**Leader:** Confessing that Jesus is Lord to the glory of God, go forth in the peace of Christ.

**All:** Thanks be to God.

*Depart in silence.*

# New Life

The passage from the Book of Isaiah was written long before Jesus was born. Isaiah told the people that someday one of God's servants would suffer for the sins of many. Jesus suffered and died to free all people from sin and to bring them back to God's friendship. That is why the Church calls Jesus the Suffering Servant.

**❓ What are some ways you can imitate the love of Jesus in word and action?**

## (ACTIVITY)

### A Flower Cross

Make flower petals out of art paper or colored tissue. Write on the flower petals some act of kindness or sacrifice that you will do during the Triduum. Glue the flowers onto a cardboard cross. Let your flower-cross be a reminder of your faith that the way of the cross leads to life.

# Light of the World

On Easter the Church celebrates Jesus' Resurrection. When Jesus was raised from the dead on the third day, he conquered the power of sin and death. The Church celebrates Easter for fifty days from Easter Sunday to Pentecost.

The Easter season is one of joy and gladness. Alleluias are sung once again. Flowers and plants fill the churches, signs of the new life Christ brings. Choirs sing Glory to God! and the altar is draped in white cloth. All are signs of the light that Jesus brings into the world.

## Light in the Darkness

In the northern hemisphere, Easter comes at a time when the darkness of winter has given way to spring. Leaves appear on trees and flowers blossom. Spring is a season of new life.

Jesus' Resurrection is a sign of the new life that bursts forth in the bright light of the sun. Jesus triumphed over the selfishness that leads people away from God. He turned the darkness of sin into the light of love. That is why Jesus is called the Light of the World.

❓ **What are some ways Jesus is light for you?**

# Celebrate Easter

## Gather

*Pray the Sign of the Cross together.*

Leader: Light and peace in Jesus Christ our Lord. Alleluia.

All: **Thanks be to God, alleluia.**

Reader: Christ is our light in the darkness!

All: **Alleluia, alleluia, alleluia.**

Reader: Christ shows us the path of love and light!

All: **Alleluia, alleluia, alleluia.**

Reader: Christ is the Way, the Truth, and the Life!

All: **Alleluia, alleluia, alleluia.**

Leader: Let us pray.

*Bow your heads as the leader prays.*

All: **Amen, Alleluia.**

## Listen to God's Word

Reader: A reading from the holy Gospel according to Matthew.

*Read Matthew 28:1–10.*
The Gospel of the Lord.

All: **Praise to you, Lord Jesus Christ.**

## Dialogue

What was your first thought as you heard this gospel?

What did Jesus tell the women?

## Blessing with Holy Water

*Step forward and bow before the Easter candle.*
*Then dip your hand in the blessed water and make*
*the Sign of the Cross.*

*Sing together the refrain.*

Alleluia, alleluia, alleluia!

"Easter Alleluia" © 1986, GIA Publications, Inc.

**Leader:** Let us pray.

*Bow your head as the leader prays.*

All: **Amen.**

# Go Forth!

**Leader:** Let us go forth and share the
good news that Christ our light
has risen! Alleluia!

All: **Thanks be to God. Alleluia!**

# Let Your Light Shine

Did you ever notice that outside on a dark night, away from the lights of the city, the stars seem brighter? In a similar way, the light of Christ brightens the darkness of the world. In the midst of sadness and violence, Christ's light shines even more brightly. In the midst of loneliness or rejection, the light of Christ's love is there to warm the heart that is hurting.

**❓ What are some things you can do to help others to know the light of Christ's love?**

## ACTIVITY
## The Light of the World

On poster board, make a Christ candle. Decorate your candle with symbols of Jesus as the Light of the World. Draw seven rays of light radiating from the candle flame. On the rays write things you and your family can do each week during the Easter season to bring Christ's light into your neighborhood and community. Share your ideas with your family.

# The Power of the Holy Spirit

The Feast of Pentecost is one of the most important celebrations of the Church. The Acts of the Apostles tell us that the followers of Jesus were gathered in Jerusalem fifty days after Easter when the Holy Spirit came to them.

## Pentecost Today

Today the Church rejoices in the Resurrection of the Lord for fifty days after Easter. Then on Pentecost, the Church celebrates the gift of the Holy Spirit to the Church. The Holy Spirit gave the first disciples the wisdom and courage they needed to preach the gospel.

The coming of the Holy Spirit marked the true beginning of the Church. From this time onward, the Church has been empowered by the Holy Spirit to spread the good news by word and action. He builds up the Church, empowers her for service, and is the source of her holiness.

❷ **How is the Holy Spirit active in the world today?**

# Celebrate Pentecost

## Gather

*Pray the Sign of the Cross together.*

**Leader:** Light and peace in Jesus Christ our Lord, alleluia.

**All:** **Thanks be to God, alleluia.**

*Sing together.*

If you believe and I believe,
And we together pray,
The Holy Spirit must come down
And set God's people free,
And set God's people free,
And set God's people free;
The Holy Spirit must come down
And set God's people free.

"If You Believe and I Believe" © 1991, GIA Publications, Inc.

**Leader:** Let us pray.

*Bow your heads as the leader prays.*

**All:** **Amen.**

## Listen to God's Word

**Reader:** A reading from the Acts of the Apostles.

*Read Acts 2:1–11.*
The Word of the Lord.

**All:** **Thanks be to God.**

## Dialogue

What are three things that happened to the disciples because of the coming of the Holy Spirit?

How can the Holy Spirit strengthen you?

## Offering of Gifts

*Sing together, "If You Believe and I Believe." As you sing, come forward in procession and place gifts for the poor at the base of the prayer table.*

### Intercessions

Leader:  Let us pray for the Church and the world, that all will be open to the power of the Holy Spirit.

*Respond to each intercession with these words.*

All:  **Send us your Spirit, O Lord.**

# Go Forth!

Leader:  May God bless us and give us the gifts of the Holy Spirit forever. And let us go forth in love and service to all God's people, alleluia.

All:  **Thanks be to God, alleluia!**

# Gifts of the Holy Spirit

Many stories in the Acts of the Apostles tell how the Holy Spirit guided the followers of Jesus to spread the good news of Jesus. The disciples told all who would listen about the life of Jesus and his commandment of love. But they lived the way of Jesus as well. You are called to do the same today.

At Baptism you received the gifts of the Holy Spirit—wisdom, understanding, right judgment, courage, knowledge, reverence, and fear of the Lord. In Confirmation you will be strengthened with these gifts.

❓ **When has the Holy Spirit helped you to use one of these gifts?**

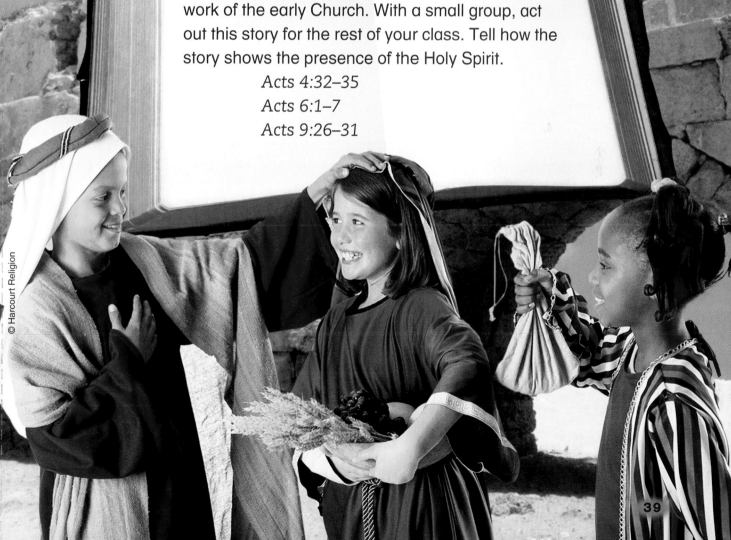

## ACTIVITY
# The Holy Spirit

Read one of the Scripture stories that describe the work of the early Church. With a small group, act out this story for the rest of your class. Tell how the story shows the presence of the Holy Spirit.

Acts 4:32–35

Acts 6:1–7

Acts 9:26–31

# UNIT 1

## God's Covenant

What do you think you will learn in this unit about God's covenant?

© Harcourt Religion

# Chapter 1 God's Plan

## Let Us Pray

**Leader:** Creator God, we thank you for your guidance.

"I will instruct you and show you the way
you should walk,
give you counsel and watch over you."

*Psalm 32:8*

**All:** Creator God, we thank you for your guidance. Amen.

## Activity   Let's Begin

**Kaleidoscope**   Have you ever looked through a kaleidoscope? As you turn the tube, small bits of colored glass or plastic at the far end are reflected in two mirrors. As you turn the kaleidoscope, the colored bits arrange themselves into thousands of beautiful patterns.

• Write a haiku—a type of poem—about the beauty of the kaleidoscope patterns on this page.

# God's Creation

 **Focus** What did God say about all that he had made?

The world is something like a kaleidoscope. Its complex patterns and movements give clues to God's amazing plan for creation. In this poem the poet imagines a powerful God who walks and talks like a man. Read to learn how the poet thinks God feels about creation.

A POEM

## The Creation

. . . And far as the eye of God could see
Darkness covered everything.
Blacker than a hundred midnights
Down in a cypress swamp.

Then God smiled,
And the light broke,
And the darkness rolled up on one side,
And the light stood shining on the other,
And God said: "That's good!"

Then God reached out and took the light
in his hands,
And God rolled the light around in his hands
Until he made the sun;
And he set that sun a-blazing in the heavens.
And the light that was left from making the sun
God gathered it up in a shining ball
And flung it against the darkness,
Spangling the night with the moon and stars.
Then down between
The darkness and the light
He hurled the world;
And God said: "That's good!"

*Then God made the seven seas and all the forests and plants and animals and even rainbows. But God decided to make even more.*

Then God sat down—
On the side of a hill where he could think;
By a deep, wide river he sat down;
With his head in his hands,
God thought and thought,
Till he thought: I'll make me a man!

Up from the bed of the river
God scooped the clay;
And by the bank of the river
He kneeled him down;
And there the great God Almighty
Who lit the sun and fixed it in the sky,
Who flung the stars to the most far corner of the night,
Who rounded the earth in the middle of his hand;
This great God,
Like a mammy bending over her baby,
Kneeled down in the dust
Toiling over a lump of clay
Till he shaped it in his own image;

Then into it he blew the breath of life,
And man became a living soul.

From the poem by James Weldon Johnson

❓ **What did you learn about God from this poem?**

## Activity — Share Your Faith

**Reflect:** In what ways does the world show God's love and care for his creation?

**Share:** With a partner, name some of these ways.

**Act:** Make a scenic postcard design of one part of the world that shows God's love and care.

# God's Plan

**Focus** Where does God reveal his plan for you?

## Faith Fact

The ancient town of Nineveh is located near the Tigris River in present-day Iraq.

God has a loving plan for creation. As God's plan unfolds, he keeps everyone and everything in his loving care. This is called **providence**. In this Bible story from the Old Testament, you will learn about Jonah, a man who tried to avoid God's plan for him.

✝ S C R I P T U R E                    **Book of Jonah**

# Jonah and the Big Fish

God told Jonah to tell the people of Nineveh, "The Lord has seen your sins. Change your sinful ways, or you are doomed!" Jonah got on a ship and sailed away to hide from the Lord.

God made a storm come up, and the ship was about to be broken to pieces. The sailors ran and found Jonah sleeping. "Pray to your God, that he may save us!" they cried. Jonah thought that God was punishing him, so he asked the sailors to throw him into the sea. As soon as they did, the sea became calm.

The Lord sent a giant fish that swallowed Jonah. Inside the fish, Jonah had some time to think, and he decided to follow the Lord. Three days later the fish spit him onto dry land. God was merciful to Jonah and also to the people of Nineveh, who listened to Jonah and changed their ways.

Based on the Book of Jonah

❓ **Why do you think Jonah tried to run from God?**

❓ **Have you ever avoided doing something that you knew you should do? What happened?**

## Following God's Plan

The story of Jonah is in the Old Testament of the Bible. The Bible, also called **Scripture**, is God's word written in human words. There are many more stories in the Old Testament that can show you how others have followed God's plan. Then, in the New Testament, you can see God's Son, Jesus, answering his Father's call perfectly. Through Jesus you can learn how you are to respond to God's plan for you. The Holy Spirit, whom Jesus sent to the Church, will help you.

## God's Revelation

God has made himself known gradually throughout history by words and deeds and the experience of people. The truth that God has told the world about himself is called **revelation**. Revelation is found in Scripture and in the Tradition of the Church.

❓ **What did Jonah do to figure out how to fit into God's plan for him?**

❓ **What do you think is God's plan for you?**

### Activity — Connect Your Faith

**Your Best Thinking** Think about quiet and beautiful places you have seen on a nature program or on another TV show. Draw in the TV screen a peaceful place where you could spend time thinking about important things. Then imagine yourself in this place, and think about God's plan for you.

© Harcourt Religion

# Psalm of Hope

 **Let Us Pray**

*Gather and begin with the Sign of the Cross.*

*Sing together the refrain.*

Guiding me, guarding me, the Lord is by my side;
guiding me, guarding me, the Lord upholds my life.

"Psalm 121" © 1988, GIA Publications, Inc.

**Leader:** Loving God, hear us today as we pray.

**Group 1:** I raise my eyes toward the mountains.
From where will my help come?
My help comes from the LORD,
the maker of heaven and earth.

**All:** *Sing refrain.*

**Group 2:** God will not allow your foot to slip.
Truly, the guardian of Israel
never slumbers nor sleeps.

**All:** *Sing refrain.*

The LORD will guard you
from all evil.
The LORD will guard your
coming and going both
now and forever.
*Sing refrain.*

Based on *Psalm 121*

**Leader:** Let us pray.
*Bow your heads as
the leader prays.*

**All:** **Amen.**

**46**

**A** **Check Understanding**   Circle True if a statement is true, and circle False if a statement is false. Correct any false statements.

1.  God's plan for people is revealed gradually.

    True        False _____

2.  Revelation is found only in creation.

    True        False _____

3.  God's plan for creation has been destroyed.

    True        False _____

4.  Providence is God's loving care for all of creation.

    True        False _____

5.  Jesus always followed God his Father's plan for him.

    True        False _____

**B** **Make Connections**   Write a brief response. What are some ways that you can learn more about God's plan for you?

_____

_____

**Activity**   Live Your Faith

**Make a Plan**   Use this calendar to list one way you will look for God and his guidance each day next week.

SUNDAY

MONDAY

TUESDAY

WEDNESDAY

THURSDAY

FRIDAY

SATURDAY

# Family Faith

## Catholics Believe

- God loves and cares for all creation and has a plan for the world.

- Everything God wants you to know about him is contained in Scripture and in the Tradition of the Church.

✝ SCRIPTURE

Read *2 Samuel 7:12–17* to learn about God's providence for the people of Israel.

**GO ONLINE** www.harcourtreligion.com
For weekly Scripture readings and seasonal resources

## Activity

# Live Your Faith

**Make a Kaleidoscope** Talk with your family about what you have learned about God's providence. Then make a kaleidoscope pattern. Cut some colored paper into shapes like the pieces of colored glass in a kaleidoscope. Give two pieces of paper to each family member. Ask each person to draw or glue pictures on the pieces that show God's loving care at work in creation. Glue the pieces to a large piece of paper to make a beautiful kaleidoscope pattern.

# People of Faith

**Mary** cooperated with God's plan. Because she did, Jesus was able to reveal fully his Father's plan for creation. Mary's "yes" to the Angel Gabriel's announcement opened the way for the Son of God's birth through the power of the Holy Spirit. Mary opened her heart to listen for the voice of God. She was a woman of prayer and stillness, always saying "yes" to God. Mary is the model of holiness for the whole Church. January 1 is the feast of Mary, the Mother of God.

▲ Mary, Mother of God

 Family Prayer

Mary, Mother of God and mother of all, help us say "yes" to God always. Show us the way of love. Amen.

© Harcourt Religion

*In Unit 1 your child is learning about REVELATION.*

**CCC** *See Catechism of the Catholic Church 80–83, 302–308 for further reading on chapter content.*

# Chapter 2 God Is Faithful

 **Let Us Pray**

**Leader:** We place our trust in your faithfulness, O God.

> "The LORD is trustworthy in every word,
> and faithful in every work."
>
> *Psalm 145:13*

**All:** We place our trust in your faithfulness, O God. Amen.

## Activity · Let's Begin

### A Very Bad Day

My day was going smooth as silk,
'Til the cat leapt up and spilled my milk.
As I was mopping up the floor,
My mom was calling from the door.
"Hurry up! We'll all be late!"
I grabbed the toast left on my plate.
Just as we reached the end of the block,
I noticed I had no left sock.
I got to school five minutes late,
I guess my toast will have to wait.
As I raced inside the classroom door,
My homework lay on the living room floor!

- What do you do when you have a
  bad day?

# Humans Choose Sin

 **Focus** How does God show his faithfulness?

For the first humans, known as Adam and Eve in the Old Testament creation story, there was a time when every day was a good day. But one day Satan, who was God's enemy, came to Eve in the form of a snake and tempted her. We learn from the Book of Genesis what Adam and Eve did.

## ✝ SCRIPTURE                                                   Genesis 3

In the Garden of Eden was one special tree that God told Adam and Eve not to touch. But Satan convinced Eve that if she and Adam ate the fruit of that tree, they could be more like God. Adam and Eve did as Satan said; but after they sinned, they felt ashamed. They learned how it felt to do something wrong.

Everything got harder for Adam and Eve. God sent them away from the garden. They had to work to find food and shelter. From then on, jealousy, sadness, and fighting were in the world.

Based on *Genesis 3*

❓ **Why do you think the first people chose to disobey God?**

## Consequences

Humans were created to share God's life and to be happy with God forever. By disobeying God, the first people broke their friendship with God. This sin of the first humans is called original sin because since that choice was made, sin has been present throughout the world. Original sin affects every human. Ignorance, the inclination to sin, suffering, and death all came into the world as a result of original sin.

Even though God sent Adam and Eve away from the garden, he did not abandon them. God remained faithful. In return he wanted all humans to be free and faithful to him, so that they could be happy forever.

The Book of Genesis then tells another famous story, the story of Noah. The point of Noah's story is that even when people continued to sin and to disobey God, God was faithful.

### Words of Faith

**Original sin** is the choice of the first humans to disobey God.

*Noah's Ark* by Malcah Zeldis

---

## Activity — Share Your Faith

**Reflect:** Think of some stories in the news that are examples of the effects of original sin in the world today.

**Share:** In a small group, talk about ways that people can act as God wants them to act in these situations.

**Act:** Write two examples here.

_____

_____

_____

_____

# God's Plan Revealed

 **Focus** What did God promise to Abram?

After a long time, God called a man named Abram to help humans remain faithful. God revealed his plan to Abram in a new way.

✝ SCRIPTURE          Genesis 12:1–8; 15:1–5; 17:5–9, 15; 21:1–3

## God Calls Abram

Abram lived long, long ago in an ancient city called Haran. God told Abram to leave his country and much of his family and go to a new land called Canaan. God told Abram, "I will bless you and make your descendants into a great nation." Abram obeyed God. He took his wife Sarai, his brother's son Lot, and all their possessions on the long journey to the new land.

Abram and his family were never alone on their difficult journey. They knew that God was always with them. Every time Abram reached a stop on the journey, he built an altar of thanksgiving to the Lord.

Many years later, after Abram had settled in the land of Canaan, the Lord spoke again to him, saying, "Don't be afraid! I will protect and reward you."

Abram replied, "Lord, you have given me everything I could ask for, except children."

The Lord told Abram, "Look at the sky and count the stars. That is how many descendants you will have."

❓ **What is something you have been asked to do that was very hard?**

# God's Covenant with Abraham

God appeared to Abram again. God made a **covenant** with Abram and his descendants for all time. God told Abram that the land of Canaan would belong to Abram and his descendants forever. He said that Abram would be the father of many nations and that these people would be God's people. As a sign of the covenant, God changed the names of Abram and his wife Sarai to Abraham and Sarah. Soon after that, even though Sarah was old, she had a son, whom the couple named Isaac.

Based on *Genesis* 12:1–8, 15:1–5, 17:5–9, 15; 21:1–3

❓ **How did Abraham and Sarah follow God's will?**

Abraham and Sarah never turned away from God. Like Abraham and Sarah, you are **faithful** to God every time you obey his laws and make loving choices.

## Common Ancestors

Abraham is considered an ancestor in faith of Christianity, Judaism, and Islam. These religions see their origins in Abraham's free response to God's revelation that he was the one God they should believe in and follow.

## Words of Faith

A **covenant** is a sacred promise or agreement between God and humans.

To be **faithful** is to be steadfast and loyal in your commitment to God, just as he is faithful to you.

**Activity** Connect Your Faith

**Show Faith** Write your first name in colorful letters. Around your name, write words that tell how you show that you are faithful to God.

# Prayer for Mercy

 Let Us Pray

*Gather and begin with the Sign of the Cross.*

*Sing together the refrain.*

God ever-faithful,
God ever-merciful,
God of your people,
hear our prayer.

"General Intercessions" © 1990,
GIA Publications, Inc.

**Leader:** For times we have failed,
we pray,

**All:** *Sing refrain.*

**Reader 1:** For people in the world
who have been hurt
by our neglect,
we pray,

**All:** *Sing refrain.*

**Reader 2:** For times when we were
unfaithful to God's
covenant of love,
we pray,

**All:** *Sing refrain.*

**Leader:** Let us pray.

*Bow your heads as
the leader prays.*

**All:** **Amen.**

**A** **Work with Words**   Fill in the blanks, using terms from the Word Bank.

**WORD BANK**

faithful
sin
Exodus
covenant
hope
names
friendship

1. By disobeying God, the first people broke their _____ with him.

2. One consequence of the disobedience of Adam and Eve is the inclination to _____.

3. God always remains _____ to his people.

4. God made a _____ with Abraham and his descendants.

5. As a sign of the covenant, God changed the _____ of Abram and Sarai.

**B** **Check Understanding**   Write one thing you have learned about God from each of the following stories.

In the Garden _____

God Calls Abram _____

## Activity — Live Your Faith

**Your Commitment**   On a separate sheet of paper, create a sign that expresses your commitment to being faithful to God's love for you. You can connect your sign with those of other group members to create a covenant banner.

# Family Faith

## ◎ Catholics Believe

- God's covenant with Abraham reveals that God is always faithful to his people.

- Sin is present in the world because of human choice.

### ✝ SCRIPTURE

Read *Genesis 13*, *Genesis 21:1–8*, or *Genesis 25:7–11* to find other stories about Abraham and Sarah.

**www.harcourtreligion.com**
For weekly Scripture readings and seasonal resources

## Activity

# Live Your Faith

**Travel Brochure** Share with your family one thing that you learned in class. Then imagine that you could visit the places where Abraham and Sarah traveled. As a family, make pages for a travel brochure that tells about their experiences. Think of the stories in this chapter. Look in a Bible to find a map of Abraham's journey. Bring your brochure to share with the group.

# People of Faith

**Naomi** was an Israelite who, because of a great famine, left her home to live among people of another land. While living in this land, she remained faithful to the God of Israel. When her husband and two sons died, she wanted to return to the land of her ancestors. Her daughter-in-law **Ruth** promised to come with her. Ruth told Naomi, "For wherever you go I will go, wherever you lodge I will lodge, your people shall be my people, and your God my God" (*Ruth 1:16*).

▲ Naomi and Ruth

##  Family Prayer

Loving God, please help us remain faithful to our covenant relationship with you, as Ruth and Naomi did. Amen.

*In Unit 1 your child is learning about* REVELATION.

**CCC** *See Catechism of the Catholic Church 59–61, 385–389 for further reading on chapter content.*

# Chapter 3 The Ten Commandments

 **Let Us Pray**

**Leader:** Loving Father, help us hear your voice and know your will.

"To do your will is my delight;
my God, your law is in my heart!"

*Psalm 40:9*

**All:** Loving Father, help us hear your voice and know your will. Amen.

© Harcourt Religion

**Activity** Let's Begin

**The Golden Eggs** There once lived a farmer and his wife who were very poor. One day, a beautiful goose strutted across their path. The woman sighed, "What a beautiful bird!"

The goose followed the couple home. The next morning, they found that the bird had laid a golden egg. Each day the goose laid yet another golden egg. Soon the couple became rich.

But the farmer grew impatient for more gold. "I will kill the goose and slice her open," he thought, "and I'll have all her eggs at once." So he cut open the goose, but inside there were no more golden eggs. And now he had no goose!

• What does this story teach you? Share your response with the group.

# Journey to Freedom

 **Focus** Who helped lead God's people to freedom?

In the story of "The Golden Eggs," the husband was a slave to greed. Here are two Bible stories about how God led his people from slavery to freedom.

© Harcourt Religion

## ✝ SCRIPTURE                    Genesis 37:1–4, 42:6–8, 44:1–12, 45:4–5

# Joseph and His Brothers

Jacob, one of Abraham's descendants, had twelve sons. Jacob's older sons hated their younger brother Joseph because he was their father's favorite.

One day Joseph's brothers threw him into a dry well. Then they sold him as a slave in Egypt. They told their father that wild animals had killed Joseph. Now more of their father's goods would belong to them.

Over the years, Joseph's power to tell the meaning of dreams won him a place of honor with Pharaoh, the leader of Egypt. During a famine, Joseph's brothers came to the court to beg for grain. The brothers did not recognize Joseph, but Joseph knew them.

To test them, Joseph had servants fill the brothers' sacks with grain and put a silver cup into the sack of his brother Benjamin. Later he had his servants follow them and discover the silver cup in the sack. Joseph then told the brothers that Benjamin was to be his slave.

Benjamin's brother Judah pleaded for him, saying that their father would be brokenhearted if Benjamin did not return. At this news, Joseph wept and told the men that he was their brother. He forgave them.

Based on *Genesis 37:1–4, 42:6–8, 44:1–12, 45:4–5*

**❓ When have you forgiven someone as Joseph did?**

## From Slavery to Freedom

When Joseph's brothers sold him as a slave, they caused problems for themselves as well. It was only when Joseph forgave his brothers that his family knew real freedom and happiness again.

SCRIPTURE                    Exodus 2:1–10, 5:1–2, 14:10–31

# The Exodus from Egypt

Many years later God's people, the Israelites, were slaves in Egypt. Their male children were being killed, so one Israelite mother hid her baby boy in a basket near the Nile River. When Pharaoh's daughter found the baby, she kept him and named him Moses. She raised him at court as her son.

When Moses grew older, God called him to be a leader of his people. God asked Moses to tell Pharaoh to stop hurting the Israelites, but Pharaoh did not listen.

Finally, Moses was able to lead the Israelites out of Egypt. At the Red Sea, Moses raised his staff and the waters parted for the Israelites to pass through.

Based on *Exodus 2:1–10, 5:1–2, 14:10–31*

❓ **Do you think it was hard for Moses to leave Pharaoh's court? Why or why not?**

**Reflect:** When have you been jealous of someone else because of his or her gifts or belongings?

**Share:** Tell a partner why you were jealous of this person and how you handled the situation.

**Act:** Imagine that you are writing a musical, and use a familiar tune to help you write a song that explains the situation.

# A Guide from God

 **Focus** How do the Ten Commandments help you be free?

The Israelites were free from slavery, but they still needed God's help.

## ✝ SCRIPTURE
Exodus 17—20

# The Journey Continues

## Words of Faith

The **Ten Commandments** are the summary of laws that God gave Moses on Mount Sinai. They tell what is necessary in order to love God and others.

After the Israelites crossed the Red Sea, they wandered in the desert for years. They forgot that God had saved them from slavery in Egypt. Moses struggled to keep order among God's people and to find food and water for them. He complained to God about his hard job, and God helped him.

In the desert, God called Moses up to Mount Sinai. After God showed his power with thunder and lightning, he gave Moses the **Ten Commandments** to show the people how they were to live.

*Based on Exodus 17—20*

❓ **Why do you think the Ten Commandments are important?**

## Living God's Covenant

Just as the Ten Commandments helped the Israelites live their covenant relationship with God, the Commandments are also a guide for you. They tell you the minimum that is required to love God and others. The first three commandments show you how to be faithful to God. The last seven show you how to treat other people with love. The chart on the next page names the Ten Commandments and explains what each one means for you.

# The Ten Commandments

| The commandment | What the commandment means |
|---|---|
| 1. I am the Lord your God. You shall not have strange gods before me. | • Place your faith in God alone.<br>• Worship, praise, and thank the Creator.<br>• Believe in, trust, and love God. |
| 2. You shall not take the name of the Lord your God in vain. | • Speak God's name with reverence.<br>• Don't curse.<br>• Never call on God to witness to a lie. |
| 3. Remember to keep holy the Lord's day. | • Gather to worship at the Eucharist.<br>• Rest and avoid unnecessary work on Sunday. |
| 4. Honor your father and your mother. | • Respect and obey your parents, guardians, and others who have proper authority. |
| 5. You shall not kill. | • Respect and protect the lives of others and your own life. |
| 6. You shall not commit adultery. | • Be faithful and loyal to friends and family.<br>• Respect God's gift of sexuality. |
| 7. You shall not steal. | • Respect the things that belong to others.<br>• Share what you have with those in need. |
| 8. You shall not bear false witness against your neighbor. | • Be honest and truthful.<br>• Do not brag about yourself.<br>• Do not say untruthful or negative things about others. |
| 9. You shall not covet your neighbor's wife. | • Practice modesty in thoughts, words, dress, and actions. |
| 10. You shall not covet your neighbor's goods. | • Rejoice in others' good fortune.<br>• Do not be jealous of others' possessions.<br>• Do not be greedy. |

## Activity  Connect Your Faith

**Commandments and You**   This week you made a number of decisions. Write down one decision you made, and tell which commandment you followed when you made that decision.

_____

_____

# Psalm of Celebration

 Let Us Pray

*Gather and begin with the Sign of the Cross.*

*Sing together the refrain.*

Sing, O people, sing our God together,
raise your voices: sing alleluia!

"Sing Our God Together" © 1993, GIA Publications, Inc.

| | |
|---|---|
| Leader: | The Lord gives us the commandments as a way of living. Let us praise God for the gift of salvation. |
| Reader 1: | Then was our mouth filled with laughter, on our lips there were songs. |
| All: | *Sing refrain.* |
| Reader 2: | What marvels the LORD worked for us! Indeed we were glad. |
| All: | *Sing refrain.* |
| Reader 3: | Those who are sowing in tears will sing when they reap. |
| All: | *Sing refrain.* |
| Reader 4: | They go out, they go out, full of tears; they come back, they come back, full of song. |
| All: | *Sing refrain.* |
| Leader: | Let us pray. |
| | *Bow your heads as the leader prays.* |
| All: | **Amen.** |

Based on *Psalm 126*

# Review and Apply

**A** **Work with Words** Match each description in Column 1 with the correct term in Column 2.

**Column 1**

_____ **1.** forgave his brothers

_____ **2.** Israelites' place of slavery

_____ **3.** leader of Egypt

_____ **4.** led Israelites to freedom

_____ **5.** some of God's laws

**Column 2**

**a.** Moses

**b.** Pharaoh

**c.** Ten Commandments

**d.** Joseph

**e.** Egypt

**B** **Check Understanding** Write these commandments. Tell a partner one way to keep each commandment.

3rd: _____

4th: _____

5th: _____

7th: _____

**Activity** Live Your Faith

**Commandment Bookmark** Design a bookmark with a saying on each side. On the front, write a way to keep one of the first three commandments. On the back, write a way to keep one of the last seven commandments. Decorate your bookmark.

Rest on Sunday

Be honest and Truthful

# Family Faith

## Catholics Believe

- God gave you the Ten Commandments to help you be faithful to him and his covenant.

- The commandments tell you ways to love God and others.

### ✝ SCRIPTURE

Read *Matthew 5:43–48* to learn about the importance of loving both friends and enemies.

**GO ONLINE** www.harcourtreligion.com
For weekly Scripture readings and seasonal resources

## Activity
# Live Your Faith

**Covenants** With your family, discuss what you learned about living God's covenant. Then write a family covenant. Begin by writing ways that you will show love and respect for one another. Then, write a promise to love God and others. Sign your names to the covenant, and display it where all can see it.

# People of Faith

▲ Aaron and Miriam c. 1800 B.C.

**Aaron** was the older brother of Moses. He assisted his brother in the Exodus from Egypt and during the years in the desert. Aaron was a high priest, responsible for the worship and sacrifice that would keep the Israelites on the path God had set for them. **Miriam** was the sister of Aaron and Moses. She is called a prophet—a person who speaks the truth to the people about God. She led the women in song and dance after the escape from Egypt.

## 🙏 Family Prayer

God our Father, help us see and follow your guidance, as Aaron and Miriam did. Give us patience on our faith journey. Amen.

*In Unit 1 your child is learning about REVELATION.*

**A** **Work with Words** Use the clues to solve the puzzle. Write the answer to each clue in the boxes. When you have finished, read down the column with the circles to find the hidden word.

1. What we call the first people's choice to disobey God

2. The summary of laws that God gave Moses

3. Said "yes" to God's will and became the Mother of Jesus

4. What Adam and Eve ate

5. God's loving care for all things; his will and plan for creation

6. How God tells humans about himself and makes his plan known

7. Steadfast and loyal in your commitment to God

8. What Joseph did after his brothers pleaded for Benjamin to be spared

9. A sacred promise or agreement between God and humans

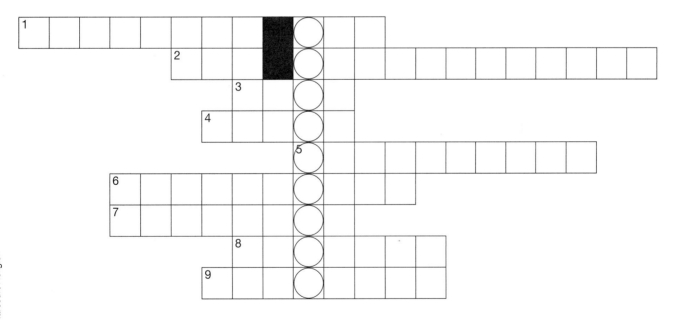

10. Hidden Word: _____ is another name for the Bible, or the word of God written in human words.

# UNIT 2
## A Faithful People

**Chapter 4**

## In God's Image

*What does it mean to be created in the image of God?*

**Chapter 5**

## Created for One Another

*Why must you love your neighbor?*

**Chapter 6**

## Making Good Choices

*What gifts from God help you make good choices?*

 **What do you think you will learn in this unit about faithful people?**

© Harcourt Religion

# Chapter 4 In God's Image

## Let Us Pray

**Leader:** God, we give you praise and thanks for all creation.
"When you send forth your breath, they are
created,
and you renew the face of the earth."

*Psalm 104:30*

**All:** God, we give you praise and thanks for all creation. Amen.

## Activity Let's Begin

### Me I Am

There is no other ME I AM

who thinks the thoughts I do;

the world contains one ME I AM,

there is no room for two.

I am the only ME I AM

this earth shall ever see;

that ME I AM I always am

is no one else but ME!

A selection from the poem by Jack Prelutsky

• What is the best thing about
being you?

© Harcourt Religion

# An Image of Love

 **Focus** What does it mean to be created in the image of God?

God has given you life. He has created you and all people to reflect his own image of love. God's image can shine in you and in every person you meet. The story of Rosa Parks teaches us that all people should be treated equally.

## Faith Fact

James Augustine Healy was the first African American Catholic bishop in the United States. He was named bishop of Portland, Maine, in 1875.

A BIOGRAPHY

# Rosa Parks

On the evening of December 1, 1955, Rosa Parks boarded a public bus in Montgomery, Alabama, and took a seat in the *white section*. The bus filled quickly, and soon there were no more seats. The driver noticed that Rosa, a black woman, was not sitting in the *colored section*. He asked Rosa to move to the back of the bus, but she refused. She did not argue. She simply did not move.

Before the 1960s, African Americans were unjustly treated because of their skin color. They were separated from the rest of society in many ways. Long after that day on the bus, Rosa Parks wrote, "Our mistreatment was just not right, and I was tired of it. I kept thinking about my mother and my grandparents, and how strong they were. I knew there was a possibility of being mistreated, but an opportunity was being given to me to do what I had asked of others."

**❓ When have you observed that someone was being treated in a certain way simply because of the color of his or her skin?**

## Created with Dignity

Rosa Parks is a true hero of the struggle for human rights in the United States. Yet she began by doing one simple thing on a day when she was tired. Rosa expressed the very basic Christian belief that all people have **dignity** because they are created in God's image.

✝ SCRIPTURE

God created man in his image;
    in the divine image he created him;
    male and female he created them.

*Genesis 1:27*

God made you with a human body, and you have a **soul** that will live forever. God gave you the ability to think, to love, and to make choices. You can make choices for human dignity every day.

Words of Faith

**Dignity** is self-worth. Every human is worthy of respect because he or she is made in the image of God.

**Soul** is the spiritual part of a human that lives forever.

### Activity — Share Your Faith

**Reflect:** Think of a time when you or someone you know showed respect or treated someone with dignity.

**Share:** Tell a partner what happened.

**Act:** List some ways you can protect the dignity of others.

_____

_____

_____

# Made to Love

**Focus** What is sin?

God created you to be united to him and to all people. Every time you act in a loving way, you deepen your connection to God and to the members of the Church, the Body of Christ. When you choose to treat someone badly, you hurt this person and the whole community of faith. You choose not to show love and respect.

## Failure to Love

**Sin** is always a failure to love. A sinful thought, word, or act also hurts your friendship with God. Sin affects you, too, and keeps you from becoming the person God wants you to be.

There are two kinds of personal sin—mortal and venial. Serious sins, such as murder, are called mortal sins. They destroy the friendship a person has with God and with others. In order for a sin to be mortal, the act must be seriously wrong, you must know that it is seriously wrong, and you must freely choose to do it anyway.

Venial sins are less serious sins. They are things that you do, such as disobeying, cheating, and lying, or bad habits that you develop, such as being lazy or dishonest. Sometimes sin is a failure to act. This is a sin of omission. An example of this would be to remain silent when someone tells a joke that makes fun of another person or group. Venial sin hurts your friendship with God and others, but it does not destroy it.

## Love and Respect

**Social sin** refers to the results of sin that can build up over time in a community or nation. One example of social sin is not allowing someone of a certain race or group to buy a house in a certain neighborhood. Rosa Parks acted against inequality and social sin. She defended her own dignity and the dignity of others.

All people are equal. Every person has dignity and is worthy of respect because he or she is made in God's image. Because he is the Son of God, Jesus is the perfect image of God. You are called to become more like Jesus and to reflect the love and care that he shows all people.

Words of Faith

**Sin** is a deliberate thought, word, deed, or omission contrary to the law of God.

**Social sin** is a sinful social structure or institution that builds up over time so that it affects the whole society.

### Activity

## Connect Your Faith

**Ask for Forgiveness**   Everybody sins, but not everybody asks for God's forgiveness. Write a personal prayer, asking God's forgiveness for some of your past actions.

# Prayer for Dignity and Respect

 **Let Us Pray**

*Gather and begin with the Sign of the Cross.*

*Sing together.*

Behold, behold, I make all things new, beginning
    with you and starting from today.
Behold, behold, I make all things new, my promise
    is true, for I am Christ the way.

"Behold, I Make All Things New" © 1994, The Iona Community,
    GIA Publications, Inc., agent

**Reader:** God of life,

**All:** **We pray for
the dignity of life.**

**Reader:** God of creation,

**All:** **We pray for the
dignity of life.**

**Reader:** God, the source of all life,

**All:** **We pray for the dignity
of life.**

**Reader:** God, the protector of
all humanity,

**All:** **We pray for the dignity
of life.**

**Leader:** God, we give you praise
and thanks for all creation.

**All:** **Amen.**

# Review and Apply

**A** **Check Understanding**   Mark each statement True or False. Correct each false statement.

1. A bully can never reflect God's image. _____

2. God is with everyone at all times in all places. _____

3. You commit a mortal sin when you cheat on a spelling test. _____

4. Rosa Parks was a victim of social sin. _____

5. Each person is unique, created by God. _____

**B** **Make Connections**   Why are all people worthy of respect?

_____

_____

_____

_____

## Activity   Live Your Faith

**Show Respect**   Like Rosa Parks, some people or groups of people do not get the respect they deserve. What advice would you give to a person who is treating someone else with little or no respect?

_____

_____

_____

_____

# Family Faith

## ◎ Catholics Believe

- Every person is worthy of respect because he or she is created in God's image.

- Each person has a soul that will live forever.

### ✝ SCRIPTURE

Read *Leviticus 19:1–18, 31–37* to learn other ways in which you can respect others and yourself and treat each person with dignity.

**GO ONLINE** **www.harcourtreligion.com**
For weekly Scripture readings and seasonal resources

## Activity
# Live Your Faith

**Inside and Outside** When we respect our own dignity and that of others, we give honor to God, who has created us in his image. Gather some paper bags and magazines. Find pictures that show how you think others see you. Glue the pictures on the outside of a bag. Then find and place pictures inside the bag that show what God sees in you. Invite each person to share the contents of the bag if he or she wishes.

# People of Faith

**Edith Stein** was a teacher, a converted Catholic, and a Carmelite nun who took the religious name Teresa Benedicta. Her life was dedicated to teaching, especially the teaching of young girls and women. During the Nazi persecution of Jews, Teresa was arrested and executed at Auschwitz. She is a model of the importance of forgiveness and reconciliation during a time of great violence. Saint Teresa's feast day is August 9.

▲ Saint Teresa Benedicta 1891–1942

## 🌸 Family Prayer

Saint Teresa, may your life be a model. Pray for us that we might learn to forgive, even our enemies. Amen.

*In Unit 2 your child is learning about the TRINITY.*

**CCC** *See Catechism of the Catholic Church 355–357, 362–366 for further reading on chapter content.*

# Chapter 5 Created for One Another

## Let Us Pray

**Leader:** We thank you, O Creator, for all the gifts we share.

"The earth is the LORD's and all it holds,
the world and those who live there."

*Psalm 24:1*

**All:** We thank you, O Creator, for all the gifts we share. Amen.

© Harcourt Reli

## Activity — Let's Begin

### The Chain of Life

The human race is a kind of chain
That binds the world as one.
We share the earth below our feet
And live beneath the sun.
Bodies, faces, voices, hands—
We each are given these.
All humans share the gift of life
And share a hope for peace.

- Who are three links in your chain
of life?

# Created to Love

 **Focus** What does love of neighbor have to do with love of God?

From the time of the first humans, people have formed groups. God's plan is for people to live together in love. This story shows how God wants people to live.

## A STORY

# HOLY GROUND

One night King Solomon noticed a man carrying sacks of wheat from one barn to another. "He must be a thief," Solomon thought. Soon a different man appeared, carrying sacks of wheat back to the original barn!

The next day Solomon called each man before him separately. To the first he said, "Why do you steal from your neighbor in the middle of the night?"

"I do not steal," the man said. "My neighbor is also my brother. He has a wife and children to feed, but he won't take any extra money from me. So every night I secretly carry wheat from my barn to his."

Solomon asked the second man the same question. The man answered, "I have a big family to help me, but my brother has to pay for help, and so he needs more wheat. He won't take it from me, so at night I secretly give the wheat to him."

Solomon said, "The holiest ground in Israel is here, where brothers love each other this much. I shall build a temple here."

From a Jewish teaching story

❓ **Why would a place where people share be a good spot for a temple?**

## Community of Love

The two brothers in the story tried to provide for each other's needs. Solomon called their land holy because he knew that God is present whenever people show their love for one another. The brothers had formed a **community** of love.

❓ **What are some other practical ways that members of a community show their love for one another?**

## The Common Good

You learned in the last chapter that God made all people in his image. You are more clearly an image of God when you reflect the love of the Holy Trinity to others.

**People who live in true communities work for the common good by**

- respecting the dignity of each person and acknowledging each person's right to freedom and self-expression, as long as others are not hurt.

- making sure that every person has a way to get the things that are necessary for life, such as food, shelter, and clothing.

- providing peace, security, and order in the community.

### Words of Faith

A **community** is a group of people who hold certain beliefs, hopes, and goals in common.

**Activity** Share Your Faith

**Reflect:** How do people in your neighborhood work for the common good?

**Share:** Tell the class about one of these activities.

**Act:** Draw something that represents this activity. Add your drawing to those of others in the class to make a collage.

77

# Christian Living

 **Focus** What does it mean to live a moral life?

## Faith Fact

According to legend, third-century twin doctors Cosmas and Damian were nicknamed "moneyless ones" because they treated anyone who was sick for free!

Each person has individual rights that are balanced with a responsibility to respect and protect the rights of others. No one has unlimited freedom or an unlimited right to the earth's goods. When everyone's rights are in balance, the kingdom of God is close at hand.

You can see a good example of this in the story of the early Christians. From this passage we learn how they lived in the years just after the Resurrection and Ascension of Jesus.

 SCRIPTURE                                    Acts 2:42–45

## The Communal Life

They devoted themselves to the teaching of the apostles and to the communal life, to the breaking of the bread and to the prayers. Awe came upon everyone, and many wonders and signs were done through the apostles. All who believed were together and had all things in common; they would sell their property and possessions and divide them among all according to each one's need.

Acts 2:42–45

*St. Lawrence Giving the Treasure of the Church to the Poor* by Bernardo Strozzi

❓ **What examples can you give of people today who live as early Christians did?**

78

## Love One Another

The early Christians formed a community based on a common faith in Jesus Christ and his message. Their faith and love are an example for you today. Faith is your "yes" to all that God has revealed. God created all men and women equal and in his image. So respect for the rights and needs of others is part of faith.

Just as you cannot live in isolation from others, so you cannot believe alone. You believe as part of a larger community of faith. As a Christian believer, you are called to live a good moral life.

## Moral Living

The Christian moral life is a way of living in right relationship with God, yourself, and others. Christian morality includes following the Ten Commandments, the teachings of Jesus, and the teachings of the Church. It also includes following the good and just laws that work for the common good.

Christian families and your parish community are places where you can learn to live the Christian moral life.

## Words of Faith

**Morality** means living in right relationship with God, yourself, and others. It is putting your beliefs into action.

A **parish** is a Catholic community with shared spiritual beliefs and worship.

## Activity — Connect Your Faith

**Service Charades**   Choose three activities you have noticed members of your parish doing for one another that show God's love (for example, sorting clothes for a rummage sale or ushering for Mass). Write the activities on three separate slips of paper. Place the papers in a container. Follow your teacher's direction.

# Prayer for Community

 Let Us Pray

*Gather and begin with the Sign of the Cross.*

*Sing together the refrain.*

Love one another. Love one another,
 as I have loved you.
Care for each other. Care for each other,
 as I care for you.

"Love One Another" © 2000, GIA Publications, Inc.

Reader 1: In this chain of life, we pray for our community.

All: **May we always respect one another.**

*Sing refrain.*

Reader 2: In the chain of this parish community, we pray for greater peace, security, and order.

All: **May we always respect one another.**

*Sing refrain.*

Reader 3: In the chain of our community gathered here, we pray for a right relationship with God, others, and ourselves.

All: **May we always respect one another.**

*Sing refrain.*

Leader: Let us pray.

*Bow your heads as the leader prays.*

All: **Amen.**

**A** **Work with Words**   Solve the crossword puzzle.

**Across**

3. We show respect for everyone's rights when we work for the _____.

5. When we show this to others, we follow God's way and live a moral life.

**Down**

1. A group of people with similar beliefs, working together toward a common goal

2. Living in right relationship with God, self, and others

4. Members of a community _____ on one another.

**B** **Make Connections**   Why does your faith in God need to be expressed with others?

_____

_____

**Activity** Live Your Faith

**Moral Choices**   With a small group, create a one-act play in which the main character makes a moral choice for others in school, on the playground, or at home. Outside of class, write the script and make copies for each character. Think of simple props and costumes. Practice your play, and perform it for your class next week.

© Harcourt Religion

# Family Faith

## ◎ Catholics Believe

- God created people for one another, and all must work for the common good. Such love of neighbor reflects the love of the Holy Trinity.

- No one can believe alone, just as no one can live alone.

## ✝ SCRIPTURE

Read the Third Letter of John for advice about how a Christian community should receive strangers.

**GO ONLINE** www.harcourtreligion.com
For weekly Scripture readings and seasonal resources

## Activity
# Live Your Faith

**Christian Actions** Read the passage about the communal life from *Acts 2:42–47*. Talk with your family about ways you could share with others as the early Christians did. List your ideas, and choose just one. After doing the action, talk about the experience. Discuss how each family member contributed to the good of others.

# People of Faith

▲ Saint John of God
1495–1550

Once a soldier and a bookseller, John of God gave his life to providing for those who were poor, homeless, or sick in body or mind. He set himself to doing things to help those in need, such as providing them with food and renting a house to give them shelter. This was the beginning of the order of the Brothers of Saint John of God. Saint John's love and care for those in need continues today. The brothers provide hospitality and care for those who are poor. Saint John's feast day is March 8.

## 🌷 Family Prayer

Saint John, pray for us that we may find the wisdom to see people in need, even when the needs are not obvious. Guide us to be generous in giving gifts, time, and possessions for the good of others. Amen.

*In Unit 2 your child is learning about the TRINITY.*

**CCC** *See Catechism of the Catholic Church 1905–1912 for further reading on chapter content.*

# Chapter 6 Making Good Choices

## Let Us Pray

**Leader:** God, give me the wisdom to make good choices.

"Teach me wisdom and knowledge,
for in your commands I trust."

*Psalm 119:66*

**All:** God, give me the wisdom to make good choices. Amen.

## Activity — Let's Begin

**Think About Choices** When you were younger, your parents made most of your choices. Now that you are older, you are able to make more choices for yourself.

• What kinds of choices does your family let you make?

• What is an important choice that you have made?

# Choices and Consequences

 **Focus** What is the proper use of free will?

You have the freedom to make choices, but all choices have consequences. In this story, Julia learns a lesson from a choice she makes.

A STORY

## Julia Decides

"Come on, Julia!" said Monica. "I really want to see the new movie at the Crosstown Cinema. I thought you wanted to see it, too."

"I do want to see it," Julia replied. "Maybe we can see it next week. My coach just called an extra soccer practice for this afternoon. I have to go."

"Well, you can go to soccer practice if you want to," said Monica. "I am going to the movie."

After Monica left, Julia got ready for practice. "I can see that movie later with my sister Lila," she thought as she tied her shoes. "Right now I have to work on my goal tending. The team is counting on me."

When Julia finally saw the movie, she enjoyed it. However, not as much as she enjoyed winning the award for most improved player at the end of the season!

❓ **What is something that happened because of Julia's choice?**

## Created with Free Will

Julia's story shows that all choices have consequences. You are responsible for your choices, too.

When God created you in his image, he gave you **free will**. With your free will, you make choices. Sometimes your choices are between right and wrong. Sometimes, as in Julia's case, they are between better and best. Whenever you make a good choice, you use God's gift of free will properly and you grow closer to God.

## A Helping Hand

God gives you many gifts to help you make good choices. God's most important gift is grace, which is the power of his own life within you. You received grace in a special way in the Sacrament of Baptism. You grow in God's grace through the sacraments, prayer, and good moral choices.

In addition to his grace, God gives you the Ten Commandments and the Church to help you. God is always helping you develop a more loving relationship with him.

### Words of Faith

**Free will** is the God-given ability to choose between good and evil.

### Activity — Share Your Faith

**Reflect:** Think of some times when your choices hurt your family or friends.

**Share:** In groups, discuss ways to make better choices.

**Act:** Imagine the next chapter in the story of Julia and Monica's friendship. Role-play what you think might happen.

# Choosing to Love

 **Focus** What is a strong conscience?

Good choices help you grow as a moral person. They build good habits and strengthen your relationship with God and others. Jesus calls us to act in ways that show love, even toward people whom we do not know. One day Jesus told this story to a scholar of the law.

✝ **SCRIPTURE** Luke 10:30–37

# The Good Samaritan

Jesus said, "A Jewish traveler going from Jerusalem to Jericho was attacked by robbers who beat, robbed, and left him on the side of the road.

"A priest saw the injured traveler and moved to the other side of the road. Later a Jewish leader came to the same place, and when he saw the traveler, he too moved to the other side of the road. Finally, a Samaritan came to the place where the traveler lay dying. Unlike the others, the Samaritan stopped. He treated and bandaged the traveler's wounds. He carried him on his own animal to an inn, where he cared for him. The next day, when the Samaritan was leaving, he gave the innkeeper money and told him, 'Take care of this man. If you spend more than what I have given you, I will repay you when I return.'"

*Based on Luke 10:30–37*

❓ **What was difficult about the choice the Samaritan made?**

❓ **When is it difficult for you to make good choices?**

# God's Gift of Conscience

Good choices strengthen your relationship with God and others. Sin weakens or destroys that relationship. Sin is always a failure to love God and others. When you use your free will to sin, you always become less free.

You probably know when you have done something wrong, even if no one has seen you. The "inner voice" that tells you so is your **conscience**. Conscience is your free will and your reason working together. They direct you to choose what is good and avoid what is wrong.

You have the seeds of a strong conscience within you. It is your job to strengthen, or form, your own conscience. You cannot do this alone.

## Words of Faith

**Conscience** is the gift from God that helps you know the difference between right and wrong and helps you choose what is right.

## FORMING YOUR CONSCIENCE

The Holy Spirit ⟷ *Strengthens you to make good choices*

Prayer and study ⟷ *Help you think things through*

Scripture and Church teaching ⟷ *Guide your decisions*

Parents, teachers, and wise people ⟷ *Give you good advice*

## Activity — Connect Your Faith

Dear Pam,

I'm invited to sleep over at my friend's house on Friday night. She has a video for us to watch. My parents already told me this video is not for children. I'm a little worried, but my friend said, "Don't be such a baby. They will never know." What should I do?

Confused

**"Dear Pam"** Imagine that you write an advice column in a newspaper. What advice would you give to help the letter-writer use God's gift of conscience?

_____

_____

_____

_____

_____

© Harcourt Religion

87

# Prayer of Reflection

 Let Us Pray

*Gather and begin with the Sign of the Cross.*

Leader: In prayer, you listen for God's voice to guide you. Close your eyes and think about a time when you were afraid and didn't know what to do. Listen to this story about a man named Elijah, who heard God's voice in a very surprising way when he was afraid.

Reader: *Read 1 Kings 19:9–14.*

Leader: Sit quietly and notice whether you can hear God whispering to you inside your heart. What is God saying to you? What do you want to say to God?

Leader: God of the whispering sound, help us be still and listen for your voice to guide us.

All: **Amen.**

*Sing together.*

For you, O Lord, my soul in stillness waits, truly my hope is in you.

"My Soul in Stillness Waits" © 1982, GIA Publications, Inc.

© Harcourt Religion

**A** **Work with Words**   Complete each sentence with the correct word from the Word Bank.

1. When God created you in his image, he gave you _____ to use in making good choices.

2. _____ is the gift from God that helps you know the difference between right and wrong.

3. Good choices help you grow as a _____ person.

4. Sin weakens or destroys your relationship with _____ and with _____.

5. Every choice you make has _____.

**B** **Make Connections**   Mark the loving choices with a heart and the unloving choices with an X.

_____ You do not finish your homework, and you lie about it.

_____ You send a card to a relative who is sick.

_____ You tell your parents when your younger brother or sister does something dangerous.

## Activity   Live Your Faith

**Make a Poster**   Steve's grandmother is watching him overnight. After she is asleep, Steve realizes that he could make a long distance call to his best friend who moved away. His grandmother would never know. What good advice would you give Steve?

• Work with a partner to design a poster.

• On the poster, write good rules for using the telephone.

Telephone Rules

# Family Faith

## Catholics Believe

- God has given you free will so that you can make good choices.

- Your conscience is the "inner voice" that helps you choose what is good.

### ✝ SCRIPTURE

*Matthew 26:69–75* is about a choice Peter made the night before Jesus died. Read the story together, and talk about the lesson it teaches.

**GO ONLINE** www.harcourtreligion.com
For weekly Scripture readings and seasonal resources

## Activity

# Live Your Faith

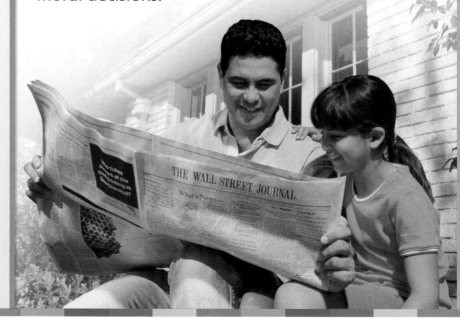

**Read Together** Read through the newspaper to find articles about people who have made good or bad moral choices. As a family, discuss how conscience guides people to make better moral decisions.

# People of Faith

▲ Saint Charles Lwanga and his companions

**Charles Lwanga** was a young servant in the king's court in Uganda. The king hated Christians. He commanded his servants to join in immoral activities. Charles, the master of the court pages, and twenty-one other young Christians refused. They were killed in 1886 for following their consciences. They prayed while they were dying. Saint Charles Lwanga and his companions are known as the African Martyrs. Their feast day is June 3.

## Family Prayer

Saint Charles, pray for us that we may follow our consciences, even when it is hard to do so. Help us learn from you the meaning of freedom. Amen.

*In Unit 2 your child is learning about the TRINITY.*

**CCC** *See Catechism of the Catholic Church 61, 69 for further reading on chapter content.*

# UNIT 2 REVIEW

**A** **Work with Words**   Write the correct word after each definition. Then find the word in the word search. Some words may be written backwards.

| | | | | | | | | | | |
|---|---|---|---|---|---|---|---|---|---|---|
| E | C | N | E | I | C | S | N | O | C |
| F | C | D | E | V | Q | T | Y | Y | L |
| O | L | N | N | P | I | U | H | T | G |
| C | M | J | E | K | E | P | S | I | R |
| I | L | M | L | I | X | U | X | N | A |
| W | D | I | G | N | I | T | Y | U | C |
| J | D | Y | P | P | V | S | K | M | E |
| C | R | E | A | T | E | I | N | M | Y |
| N | J | E | Z | Q | M | U | S | O | A |
| X | V | Z | O | O | R | E | S | C | C |

1. God's own life within you _____

2. To make something from nothing _____

3. The inner voice that helps you know right from wrong

   _____

4. A group of people with common beliefs and goals

   _____

5. A person's self-worth and respect _____

**B** **Check Understanding**   Match each description in Column 1 with the correct term in Column 2. Terms may be used more than once.

**Column 1**

_____ 6. Cheating on homework

_____ 7. Staying silent while someone is being teased

_____ 8. Lying to a friend

_____ 9. Choosing friends by the color of their skin

_____ 10. Murder

**Column 2**

a. mortal sin

b. venial sin

c. sin of omission

d. social sin

# UNIT 3
## Life in Christ

### Chapter 7
# You Are Blessed!
*How can you be a blessing for others?*

### Chapter 8
# The Great Commandment
*What can Jesus' Great Commandment teach you?*

### Chapter 9
# Honoring God
*What do the second and third commandments teach?*

**What do you think you will learn in this unit about life in Christ?**

# Chapter 7 You Are Blessed!

## Let Us Pray

**Leader:** All glory to you, God!

"Praise the LORD, who is so good;
God's love endures forever."

*Psalm 136:1*

**All:** All glory to you, God! Amen.

## Activity    Let's Begin

**Be Blessed**   You may have heard someone say, "We are so blessed!" Some people think of prizes, gifts, or lots of money as blessings. Others think of good health, the love of family, or the joy of good times with friends.

• What do you think it means to be blessed?

© Harcourt Religion

# True Happiness

 **Focus** What does it mean to be a blessing for others?

In this retelling of a famous story, happiness is spread by unlikely partners.

A STORY

# THE HAPPY PRINCE

High above the city, on a tall column, stood the statue of the Happy Prince. He was gilded all over with thin leaves of gold; for eyes he had two bright sapphires, and a large red ruby glowed in his sword-hilt.

One evening, a tiny swallow that was flying south stopped to rest in the statue's shadow. She looked up and saw tears coming from the prince's eyes.

"Why are you weeping?" the swallow asked. "I thought you were the Happy Prince!"

"When I was alive," answered the statue, "anything sad was hidden from me. But now I look down and see all of the city's pain.

"Look! There is a poor seamstress working on a beautiful gown for the queen. Her little boy has a fever. He would like oranges, but she has only river water to give him. Will you take her the ruby from my sword?" The swallow hesitated but then agreed.

"Just this once!" she said.

❓ **Why do you think the swallow agreed to stay and help the prince?**

# THE PRICE OF HAPPINESS

Each day, the prince convinced the swallow to stay on. Together, they gave away all the riches the prince had, including his sapphire eyes and the leaves of gold covering his garments.

When winter came, the swallow soon died from the cold. City leaders melted down the statue to make something else from it. But when they did, its heart would not burn! The prince's heart and the dead swallow ended up side by side in a trash heap.

God looked down one day from heaven and said to an angel, "Bring me the two most precious things in the city." The angel brought him the prince's heart and the dead bird.

"You have chosen well," said God, "for in my kingdom of heaven this little bird shall sing forevermore, and the Happy Prince shall praise me."

## Activity — Share Your Faith

**Reflect:** How does the Happy Prince know who needs help?

**Share:** By the end of the story, who is blessed? Discuss your response with a partner.

**Act:** Describe one way that you can be a blessing for others.

_____

_____

_____

# Jesus Brings God's Blessing

 **Focus** What did Jesus teach about the true meaning of happiness?

"The Happy Prince" tells who the writer believed would be blessed by God. In this Bible story, Jesus taught about who is blessed and how to be a blessing for others.

## ✚ SCRIPTURE                    Matthew 5:1–10

# The Sermon on the Mount

One day Jesus stood in the midst of his Apostles and a great crowd of followers. He taught them with these words:

"Blessed are the poor in spirit,
    for theirs is the kingdom of heaven.

Blessed are they who mourn,
    for they will be comforted.

Blessed are the meek,
    for they will inherit the land.

Blessed are they who hunger and thirst
      for righteousness,
    for they will be satisfied.

Blessed are the merciful,
    for they will be shown mercy.

Blessed are the clean of heart,
    for they will see God.

Blessed are the peacemakers,
    for they will be called children of God.

Blessed are they who are persecuted
      for the sake of righteousness,
    for theirs is the kingdom of heaven."

From *Matthew 5:1–10*

# The Beatitudes

The Church calls this teaching of Jesus the **Beatitudes**. The word *beatitude* means "blessing" or "happiness." The Beatitudes tell you how to be a blessing for others so that you, too, will be blessed by God. They are about the lasting happiness that God calls you to have. God desires all people to work for his kingdom and to share in eternal life with him.

## Words of Faith

The eight **Beatitudes** are teachings of Jesus that show the way to true happiness and tell the way to live in God's kingdom now and always.

Blessed are the poor in spirit . . .
Depend on God, not on material things.

Blessed are the meek . . .
Be gentle and humble with others.

Blessed are the merciful . . .
Forgive others and ask their forgiveness.

Blessed are the peacemakers . . .
Work to bring people together. Look for ways to solve problems peacefully.

Blessed are they who mourn . . .
Share other people's sorrows and joys.

Blessed are those who hunger and thirst for righteousness . . .
Help all people treat others justly, and help change unjust conditions.

Blessed are the clean of heart . . .
Be faithful to God and to God's ways.

Blessed are those who are persecuted for the sake of righteousness . . .
In difficult times, trust in God and stand up for what is right.

## Activity Connect Your Faith

**A Blessing Scene** On a separate sheet of paper, draw a picture of what you have done to live one of the Beatitudes.

# Prayer of Blessing

 Let Us Pray

*Gather and begin with the Sign of the Cross.*

Leader: Brothers and sisters, praise God, who is rich in mercy.

All: **Blessed be God forever.**

Reader 1: *Read Philippians 4:4–7.*

All: **Blessed be God forever.**

Reader 2: Loving God, you created all the people of the world, and you know each of us by name.

All: **Blessed be God forever.**

Reader 3: We thank you for our lives. Bless us with your love and friendship.

All: **Blessed be God forever.**

Reader 4: May we grow in wisdom, knowledge, and grace.

All: **Blessed be God forever.**

Leader: May we be blessed in the name of the Father, the Son, and the Holy Spirit.

All: **Amen.**

*Sing together.*

For your gracious blessing,
for your wondrous word,

for your loving kindness,
we give thanks, O God.

"For Your Gracious Blessing" Traditional

WE RECYCLE

© Harcourt Religion

**A** **Work with Words**   Complete the following paragraph with the correct words from the Word Bank.

Jesus gave us the _____ to help us be a _____ for others. As we share our blessings with others, we help them find true _____.

Through the _____ Beatitudes, Jesus tells us about being blessed by God and finding true happiness. Some of the people who are blessed are those who are

_____ , _____ ,

_____ , and _____ .

**WORD BANK**

blessing
peacemakers
poor
happiness
eight
Beatitudes
merciful
meek

**B** **Make Connections**   After studying this chapter, what other ways would you add to the definition of being blessed that you discussed on the Invite page?

_____

## Activity — Live Your Faith

**Beatitude News**   Use the five Ws—*Who, What, Where, When,* and *Why*—to write a newspaper article that shows people in your family or neighborhood living a Beatitude as they participate in an event.

My article will be titled: _____

_____

_____

_____

# Family Faith

## ◎ Catholics Believe

- The Beatitudes are eight teachings that describe the reign of God that Jesus announced when he lived on earth.

- The Beatitudes show you how to live and act as a follower of Jesus.

### ✝ SCRIPTURE

Read *Luke 6:20–26* to find out about the Beatitudes in the Gospel according to Luke.

**www.harcourtreligion.com**
GO ONLINE For weekly Scripture readings and seasonal resources

## Activity

# Live Your Faith

**Blessing Chart** Work at being a blessing. Make a chart titled "A Blessing for Others" to display in your home. Write each family member's name below the title. Each time you notice someone in the family living one of the Beatitudes, draw a heart next to his or her name. You can also write a word next to the name to tell the goodness that person showed.

# People of Faith

**Martin** was born in Lima, Peru. His father was Spanish, and his mother was a freed black slave from Panama. Martin became a Dominican brother and spent his life doing simple good works for those in need. He went throughout the city, caring for those who were sick and poor. He was a blessing to all he met, even animals. Because he was meek and pure of heart, he saw that the simplest work gave honor to God if it served others.

▲ Saint Martin de Porres 1575–1639

##  Family Prayer

Saint Martin, help us do good for those in need. Give us strength to follow your example and live for others. Amen.

*In Unit 3 your child is learning about JESUS CHRIST.*

# Chapter 8 The Great Commandment

 **Let Us Pray**

**Leader:** Merciful God, help us know and do your will.

"LORD, teach me the way of your laws;
I shall observe them with care."

*Psalm 119:33*

**All:** Merciful God, help us know and do your will. Amen.

## Activity Let's Begin

**Signs of Love**  Elena keeps a photo album. Some of the pictures are of times and places in which she showed God's love to others. Other pictures show ways that other people showed God's love to her.

• If this were your album, what picture would you show of yourself?

I was very sick today. Mom brought me food in bed.

My friends and I helped gather clothes for the needy.

GIRLS   BOYS

CLOTHING DRIVE

# Following Jesus

 **Focus** How is the Great Commandment like the Ten Commandments?

Elena and her family follow Jesus by sharing their love with others. Once, Jesus asked a young man to show his love for others in a very generous way.

## ✝ SCRIPTURE                                    Matthew 19:16–22

# The Rich Young Man

One day when Jesus was teaching, a young man asked, "What must I do to live forever with God?"

Jesus answered, "Keep the commandments."

"Which commandments?" the young man asked. Jesus listed some of the Ten Commandments for him.

"I keep all those commandments!" the young man said happily. "What else do I need to do?"

"If you really wish to be perfect," Jesus said, "go and sell everything you have. Give the money to people who are poor. Then come and follow me."

The young man's smile faded, for he was very rich. He could not imagine giving everything away, so he went away sad.

Based on *Matthew 19:16–22*

Jesus asked the rich young man to make a very big sacrifice. He knew that the young man's love for his possessions could keep him from loving God completely. When Jesus tested the young man to see how important his possessions were, the young man could not part with them.

❓ **What possession would be the hardest for you to give away? Why?**

# The Great Commandment

Jesus taught that keeping the Ten Commandments includes more than checking off items on a list. Each commandment shows you a way to love God and love others with your whole heart and soul.

### ✝ SCRIPTURE

"You shall love the Lord, your God, with all your heart, with all your soul, and with all your mind. This is the greatest and the first commandment. The second is like it: You shall love your neighbor as yourself. The whole law and the prophets depend on these two commandments."

Based on *Matthew 22:37–40*

Therefore, the **Great Commandment** sums up the Ten Commandments, the whole law, and what the prophets taught.

## Words of Faith

The **Great Commandment** is the twofold command to love God above all and your neighbor as yourself.

## Activity — Share Your Faith

Believe

**Reflect:** Look at an advertisement in a magazine. Does this ad support the teaching of Jesus?

**Share:** Share your response with a partner.

**Act:** As a group, write an ad that supports the teaching of Jesus.

# Love in Action

 How can you live the Great Commandment?

The command to love is not a weak or soft bit of advice, as this tale makes clear.

## A FOLKTALE

## *The Paper Dragon*

Long ago, a Chinese artist named Mi Fei was asked by his people to defend them against Sui Jen, a dragon. "Who dares to disturb me?" roared the dragon.

"I am Mi Fei," whispered the artist. "Spare our people."

The dragon's red eyes glowed. "Before I will do that, Mi Fei, you must perform three tasks. What is the most important thing your people have discovered?"

"I think it is paper," exclaimed Mi Fei.

"Ridiculous!" snorted the dragon. "Bring me fire, then, wrapped in paper, or I will destroy you!" After much thought, Mi Fei brought the dragon a paper lantern with a candle glowing inside.

Next, the dragon asked Mi Fei to bring the wind captured by paper. Mi Fei brought a paper fan.

The dragon gave Mi Fei his third task. "Bring me the strongest thing in the world, carried in paper." Mi Fei thought and thought. Then he painted all the loving people of his village. He returned, showed his painting, and said, "Love can move mountains; love brings light and life."

Suddenly, Sui Jen began to shrink. "Mi Fei," he said, "truly, the strongest thing in the world is love." When Mi Fei looked down, he found a small paper dragon.

❓ **What is the message of this story?**

## Jesus Shows the Way

"The Paper Dragon" is only a folktale. However, it makes the very important point that the power of love can make a difference. God the Father sent his Son to show all people how to live in love as Mi Fei did. Jesus cared most for those who were poor, helpless, and suffering, and he calls all of his followers to do the same.

## Acts of Charity

With the strength of the Holy Spirit, whom Jesus sent, you have the power to reach out to others in love, just as Jesus did. The Holy Spirit breathed **charity** into you at your baptism.

Jesus' Great Commandment tells you to love others as you love yourself. Christians see the needs of others and help meet those needs. The Church has named seven acts of kindness that you can do to meet the physical needs of others. They are called the **Corporal Works of Mercy**.

### Words of Faith

**Charity** is the virtue of love. It directs people to love God above all things and their neighbor as themselves for the love of God.

The **Corporal Works of Mercy** are actions that meet the physical needs of others.

## Activity — Connect Your Faith

**Recognize Works of Mercy** Draw lines to match each Corporal Work of Mercy with an action. Then circle the actions that you have done.

| Works of Mercy | Actions |
| --- | --- |
| Clothe the naked. | Volunteer to help serve a meal at a shelter. |
| Shelter the homeless. | Attend a funeral. |
| Feed the hungry. | Donate clothes to those in need. |
| Give drink to the thirsty. | Donate books to a prison. |
| Visit the imprisoned. | Visit a homebound relative. |
| Visit the sick. | Donate money to a homeless shelter. |
| Bury the dead. | Set up a free lemonade stand on a hot summer day. |

© Harcourt Religion

# Celebration of the Word

 **Let Us Pray**

*Gather and begin with the Sign of the Cross.*

Leader: God of Mercy, we gather to remind ourselves of your love and mercy.

Reader 1: A reading from the First Letter to the Corinthians.
*Read 1 Corinthians 13:2–7.*
The word of the Lord.

All: **Thanks be to God.**

Reader 2: Lord, give us the gift of patience.

All: **We want to live in your love.**

Reader 3: Lord, give us the gift of kindness.

All: **We want to live in your love.**

Reader 4: Lord, help us think of others.

All: **We want to live in your love.**

Leader: Let us pray.
*Bow your heads as the leader prays.*

All: **Amen.**

*Sing together.*

Ubi caritas et amor,
ubi caritas Deus ibi est.
Live in charity and steadfast love,
live in charity;
God will dwell with you.

"Ubi Caritas/Live in Charity" © 1979, Les Presses de Taizé, GIA Publications, Inc., agent

# Review and Apply

**A** **Check Understanding**  Mark each statement True or False. Correct each false statement.

1.  The Corporal Works of Mercy make it hard for you to grow as a Christian. _____

2.  Only adults have the ability to care for and help others. _____

3.  The Great Commandment is a law of love.

    _____

4.  The Great Commandment can be restated in this way: "First love God; then love others as you love yourself." _____

5.  The virtue of charity helps you perform the Corporal Works of Mercy. _____

**B** **Make Connections**  Explain why this statement is true: When you live the Great Commandment, you are living the Ten Commandments. _____

_____

© Harcourt Religion

**Activity** **Live Your Faith**

**In Jesus' Footsteps**  Followers of Jesus try to walk in his footsteps day by day, continuing his works of love and kindness. On the path below, write one way in which you will try to show your love for God and others on each day next week.

**107**

# Family Faith

## ◎ Catholics Believe

- The Great Commandment is to love God with all your heart, strength, and mind and to love your neighbor as yourself.
- The Great Commandment sums up all of the teachings of the Ten Commandments.

### ✝ SCRIPTURE

Read *Isaiah 58:6–10* and *Matthew 25:34–40* to find the Corporal Works of Mercy in the Bible.

**www.harcourtreligion.com**
For weekly Scripture readings and seasonal resources

## Activity

# Live Your Faith

**Acts of Love** Design a greeting card, and make a special family food. Deliver both to someone who is sick, elderly, or a new parent or neighbor. Spend time visiting. On the way home, talk about the experience and how it felt to live the Great Commandment.

# People of Faith

▲ Saint Katharine Drexel 1858–1955

**Katharine Drexel** devoted her money and her life to those who were poor. She did missionary work among African Americans and Native Americans. She founded the Sisters of the Blessed Sacrament to help educate members of these ethnic groups. Katharine also established many schools on Native American reservations and the first and only Catholic university for African Americans. Saint Katharine's feast day is March 3.

##  Family Prayer

Saint Katharine, pray for us that we may follow the way of Jesus. Help us live out the Corporal Works of Mercy in our daily lives. Amen.

© Harcourt Religion

*In Unit 3 your child is learning about JESUS CHRIST.*

# Chapter 9 Honoring God

Let Us Pray

**Leader:** We praise and honor your holy name, O Lord.

"Then call on me in time of distress;
I will rescue you, and you shall honor me."

*Psalm 50:15*

**All:** We praise and honor your holy name, O Lord. Amen.

## Activity — Let's Begin

**A Place of Honor** "What are you building?" Jeremy asked. "A spice rack?"

"No," said Vernique. "It's something for the whole family. It's a place of honor."

Jeremy was doubtful. "What does that mean? It just looks like a shelf."

"It's a place to put things that make us proud of our family," Vernique replied. "It's for Dad's bowling trophy and my science fair certificate—and Mom's picture that shows her shaking hands with the mayor."

"Can I put the pottery bowl I made there, too?"

"Sure," said Vernique.

• What would you put in a place of honor for your family?

# God's People Forget

**Focus** What does it mean to praise and honor God?

The ancient laws that God gave the Israelites through Moses are known as the Mosaic Law.

God created each person to be unique. God also created all humans to be alike in a most important way. He created everyone in his own image. Once, the Hebrew people forgot to show God the honor and respect that was due to the giver of such a gift.

## ✝ SCRIPTURE                                    Exodus 32:1–20

### The Golden Calf

**M**oses was with God on Mount Sinai for forty days and forty nights. When the people became aware of Moses' delay, they gathered around Aaron and said to him, "Come, make us a god who will be our leader; as for the man Moses who brought us out of the land of Egypt, we do not know what has happened to him." Aaron collected all their gold and melted it down to be formed into a golden calf. Then Aaron built an altar before the calf and declared a feast. The people brought sacrifices and worshiped the calf, saying: "This is your God, O Israel, who brought you out of the land of Egypt."

God then told Moses to return to the people and tell them how angry he was. Moses returned to the camp and destroyed the calf, turning it to powder.

Based on *Exodus 32:1–20*

❓ **Why do you think the people made the golden calf?**

❓ **Why was Moses upset?**

## Honoring God

The sin of God's people occurred while Moses was receiving the stone tablets of the Ten Commandments from God. The first commandment says, "I am the Lord your God. You shall not have strange gods before me."

The first commandment requires you to honor and worship only God. **Worship** is the adoration and praise that is due to God. You worship God when you celebrate Mass with your parish community, when you pray, and when you live a life that puts God first. Worshiping an object or a person instead of God, as the people worshiped the golden calf, is called **idolatry**.

When you worship God, you show your belief in him as the source of creation and salvation. You show that you, and all creatures, rely on him for life. You show your trust and hope in him. This is why fortune-telling or thinking that we can control nature and know the things that God knows are against the first commandment.

❓ **What are some things that people sometimes place ahead of God?**

### Words of Faith

To **worship** God is to adore and praise God, especially in prayer and liturgy.

**Idolatry** is the sin of worshiping an object or a person instead of God. It is letting anything or anyone become more important than God.

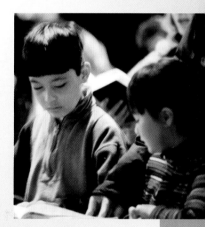

## Activity — Share Your Faith

**Reflect:** In what ways do you worship God?

**Share:** Share your responses with a partner.

**Act:** Choose the type of worship that means the most to you. Then write a few sentences explaining why this is your favorite way to worship.

_____

_____

_____

© Harcourt Religion

# Respect for God

 **Focus** What do the second and third commandments tell you to do?

The second commandment is connected to the first: "You shall not take the name of the Lord in vain." God's name is sacred, or holy, because God is sacred. When God called Moses to be the leader of his people, God revealed his name to Moses. God shared his name with his people because he loved and trusted them. In return, God's people are to bless and praise God's holy name.

This commandment calls you to always use the name of God with reverence and respect. Respecting God's name is a sign of the respect God deserves. It is a sin against God's name to curse or to use God's name to swear to a lie. To seriously dishonor the name of God, Jesus Christ, Mary, or the saints in words or actions is called **blasphemy**.

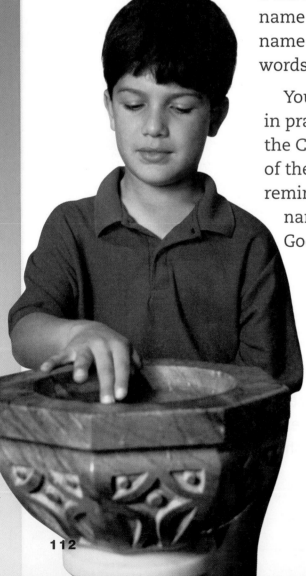

You probably use God's name most often in prayer. Every time you make the Sign of the Cross, you call on the name of the Father, of the Son, and of the Holy Spirit. This is a reminder of your baptism. Calling on God's name strengthens you to live as a child of God and a follower of Christ.

The second commandment also reminds us that God calls each person by name. A person's name is a sign of that person's dignity. You are to use the names of others with respect.

❷ **What are some ways you use God's name?**

❷ **How can you show others that you respect their names?**

## Keeping the Lord's Day

Following the first, second, and third commandments helps you love God and grow closer to him. The third commandment teaches you to honor God by celebrating Sunday, the greatest and most special day of the week for Christians. The third commandment is this: Remember to keep holy the Lord's day.

Sunday is the first day of the week. Jesus rose from the dead on the first day of the week. This is why Sunday is known as the Lord's day. Gathering on Sunday for the Eucharist has been the center of the Church's life since the time of the Apostles. This is because Sunday is the day of the Lord's Resurrection.

© Harcourt Religion

### Words of Faith

**Blasphemy** is the sin of showing contempt for the name of God, Jesus Christ, Mary, or the saints in words or actions.

### The Lord's Day

- Participate in the Sunday celebration of the Eucharist. This is the most important way to observe the third commandment.

- Rest and enjoy time with your family. Share a meal, read the Bible, or visit a relative you do not often see.

- Take part in parish activities, visit a retirement center, visit people in the community who are sick, or perform a work of service as a family.

- Respect the rights of others to rest and observe Sunday.

### Activity    Connect Your Faith

**Sunday Suggestions**    What are three other actions that you could take to remember the Lord's day?

_____

_____

_____

# Prayer of Praise

 Let Us Pray

*Gather and begin with the Sign of the Cross.*

 *Sing together.*

> Sing, sing, praise and sing! Honor God for
> ev'rything.
> Sing to God and let it ring. Sing and praise
> and sing!

"Sing, Sing, Praise and Sing!" © 2000, GIA Publications, Inc.

**Leader:** Respond to each name of God by praying:
We praise your name, O God.

**Reader:** God, our Father,

**All:** **We praise your name, O God.**

**Reader:** All merciful and gracious God,

**All:** **We praise your name, O God.**

**Reader:** God, our Creator,

**All:** **We praise your name, O God.**

**Reader:** Compassionate God,

**All:** **We praise your name, O God.**

**Reader:** God, source of all life,

**All:** **We praise your name, O God.**

**Leader:** Let us pray.
*Bow your heads as
the leader prays.*

**All:** **Amen.**

© Harcourt Religion

# Review and Apply

**A** **Check Understanding**  Mark each statement True or False. Correct each false statement.

1.  Worshiping things, or idols, is just as good as worshiping God. _____

2.  God created all humans in his own image.

    _____

3.  You can respect God and his works by not saying his name in an angry way. _____

4.  If you are truly holy in spirit, you do not need to worship at Sunday Mass. _____

5.  Following the Ten Commandments helps you grow closer to God. _____

**B** **Make Connections**  Write two ways to keep the first commandment.

_____

_____

Write two ways to keep the second commandment.

_____

_____

## Activity  Live Your Faith

**Write a Story**  Think about some events that occur within your family. Which ones bring people together? Write a short story that tells how one of these events strengthens your family's respect for God.

# Family Faith

## Catholics Believe

- The first three commandments teach you to honor God above all else, respect his name, and worship him on Sunday.

- These commandments tell you to believe in, trust, and love God.

### ✝ SCRIPTURE

Read *Psalm 119:33–48* to discover the joy you can experience by following Christ's example and living by God's law.

**GO ONLINE** www.harcourtreligion.com
For weekly Scripture readings and seasonal resources

## Activity

# Live Your Faith

**Praise God** When we perform actions that show our understanding of the first three commandments, we strengthen our love for God.

- Make a list of seven actions that you and your family can do this week to praise and honor God.
- Check off the actions as you and your family move through the week, but feel free to perform these actions more than once. No one can show too much love for God.

# People of Faith

▲ Saint Jane Frances de Chantal
1572–1641

Jane Frances de Chantal was born into a noble family in France. She married and had seven children. When Jane became a widow, she devoted herself to the religious life. She met Francis de Sales in 1604 and grew spiritually under his guidance. Eventually, Jane founded the Order of the Visitation. These women cared for those in need. Saint Jane's feast day is December 12.

## 🙌 Family Prayer

Saint Jane, pray for us that we may be respectful of the dignity of others and of our own dignity. Amen.

*In Unit 3 your child is learning about JESUS CHRIST.*

# UNIT 3 REVIEW

**A** **Work with Words** Match each description in Column 1 with the correct term in Column 2.

| Column 1 | Column 2 |
|---|---|
| _____ **1.** Loving your neighbor as yourself | **a.** Beatitudes |
| _____ **2.** The meaning of "beatitude" | **b.** charity |
| _____ **3.** The sin of showing contempt for the name of God, Jesus Christ, Mary, or the saints in words or actions | **c.** second part of the Great Commandment |
| _____ **4.** Sunday, which is the day Jesus rose from the dead | **d.** worship |
| _____ **5.** Loving God with all your heart | **e.** blessing |
| _____ **6.** Actions that care for the physical needs of others | **f.** Corporal Works of Mercy |
| _____ **7.** These tell the way to live in God's kingdom now and always. | **g.** idolatry |
| _____ **8.** To adore and praise God, especially in prayer and liturgy | **h.** Lord's day |
| _____ **9.** The virtue of love | **i.** first part of the Great Commandment |
| _____ **10.** The sin of worshiping an object or a person instead of God | **j.** blasphemy |

# UNIT 4
## The Church Teaches

**Chapter 10**

# Called to Love

*What is the Christian vocation?*

**Chapter 11**

# Models of Faith

*What makes a person holy?*

**Chapter 12**

# The Church Teaches

*What is the magisterium of the Church?*

What do you think you will learn in this unit about what the Church teaches?

© Harcourt Religion

# Chapter 10 Called to Love

 **Let Us Pray**

**Leader:** God of love, we gladly serve and obey you.

"Praise, you servants of the Lord,
    praise the name of the Lord."
*Psalm 113:1*

**All:** God of love, we gladly serve and obey you. Amen.

## Activity — Let's Begin

**Miss Rumphius** In the story *Miss Rumphius,* a young girl named Alice Rumphius is challenged by her grandfather to make the world more beautiful. Many years later, the adult Alice discovers the lupine flower. She decides to make the fields and neighborhoods of her town more beautiful. Alice walks through the town and its fields, dropping lupine seed along her way. Now those empty lots and fields are carpets of blue every spring.

• What kinds of things would make the world around you a better place? How could you help?

# God's Call

 **Focus** What does it mean to have a vocation?

Everyone has a **vocation**. A vocation is God's call to love and serve him and others. Sometimes God calls a person to a special role.

Once, long before Jesus was born, there was a young man who lived in the tiny kingdom of Judah, where the nation of Israel is today. His name was Jeremiah, which means "the Lord raises up." Jeremiah was called by God to speak the truth to his people in a time of great danger. They had lost their way and were being invaded by powerful nations. This is how Jeremiah remembered God calling him.

✝ S C R I P T U R E                          Jeremiah 1:5–8

## The Call of Jeremiah

"Before I formed you in the womb I knew you,
    before you were born I dedicated you, a
    prophet to the nations I appointed you.

Ah, Lord God! I said,
    I know not how to speak; 'I am too young.'

But the Lord answered me,
Say not, I am too young. . . .
whatever I command you, you shall speak.
Have no fear before them,
    because I am with you to deliver you."

From *Jeremiah 1:5–8*

❷ **Have you ever felt that God wanted you to do something or to make a certain choice?**

❷ **How did you know?**

© Harcourt Religion

120

## The Kingdom of God

Not everyone hears God's call as clearly as Jeremiah did. Sometimes it takes many years of praying and listening to know your vocation. It will be yours alone because you are a unique child of God.

All vocations can be ways of making the **kingdom of God** more visible. God's reign is the world of love, peace, and justice that God intends. Jesus announced the reign of God and revealed it in his life and ministry. But the reign of God will not be here fully until the end of time. Every person must help God increase his reign.

❓ **What signs can you see of God's kingdom in the world now?**

## Ways to Serve God

The Catholic Church recognizes three special ways in which people respond to God's call to serve: through the priesthood, through consecrated religious life, and through married life. Consecrated religious life is a state of life in which a person usually makes vows, or promises, of holiness.

### Words of Faith

A **vocation** is God's call to love and serve him and others.

The **kingdom of God** is God's rule of peace, justice, and love that is here now but has not yet come in its fullness.

---

**Activity** — Share Your Faith

**Reflect:** Imagine that you are much older and that a film director is preparing a movie of your life.

**Share:** Work with a partner, and pretend that your partner is the film director. Suggest two scenes that he or she could shoot to show you helping increase God's reign.

**Act:** Choose one of the scenes you described, and draw it. After you have finished drawing, write a caption for the picture.

# Serving the Church

**Focus** How do Christians help God increase his reign?

## Faith Fact

Since the Church began, the laity had important leadership roles, including teaching and missionary work.

The Church recognizes that some people may choose to serve God by remaining single rather than choosing the priesthood, religious life, or married life. Single life is also a vocation. Both single and married people are part of the **laity**.

All who are baptized can choose to serve the Church and the parish community. Here are some of their special roles.

## Many Gifts

- The pastor and pastoral associate lead and serve the parish community.
- The permanent deacon is ordained to assist the pastor, especially at Eucharist, marriages, and funerals, and to perform works of charity.
- The reader proclaims the word of God at the Liturgy of the Word.
- The extraordinary minister of Holy Communion helps distribute Holy Communion at Mass and takes Holy Communion to those who are sick or housebound.
- Altar servers assist the priest at Mass by carrying the sacramentary, the sacred vessels, and the cross.
- Musicians lead the assembly in sung prayer.
- Catechists teach Scripture and the Catholic faith to members of the parish.

❓ Who in your family has served in one of these special roles?

❓ What other roles are there? How could you share your gifts in one of these roles?

## Using Your Gifts

It can take many years to recognize your vocation in life. However, even while you are young you can use your gifts from God to make a difference. Here is the story of a boy who uses his talent to bring a powerful message to the world.

### A BIOGRAPHY

# Heartsongs

Mattie Stepanek was born with a rare form of muscular dystrophy. Although he uses a wheelchair and needs a machine to help him breathe, Mattie writes beautiful poetry.

Writing poetry helped Mattie find what he called his heartsong. "Your heartsong is your inner beauty," says Mattie. "It's the song in your heart that wants you to help make yourself a better person, and to help other people do the same. Everybody has one."

## Finding Your Heartsong

Discovering your vocation is a lot like finding your heartsong. It is finding the unique way that God wants you to make the world a better place. Everyone who brings love, peace, and justice to the world helps God increase his reign.

**Activity** Connect Your Faith

**Your Heartsong**
What could your heartsong be? Write and decorate its title in this space.

# Meditation on Peace

 Let Us Pray

*Gather and begin with the Sign of the Cross.*

Leader: Let us sit and listen to the words of the Letter to the Colossians.

Reader 1: *Read Colossians 1:2–5.*

*Silence*

*Sing together.*

Take, O take me as I am; summon out what I shall be; set your seal upon my heart and live in me.

"Take, O Take Me As I Am" © 1994, Iona Community, GIA Publications, Inc., agent

Reader 2: Let us reflect on peace and listen to words that Mattie Stepanek wrote about peace.

"I cannot wait to become

A peacemaker.

I cannot wait to help

The world overcome

Anger, and problems of evil."

What good things are you eager to do for the world?

Leader: Let us pray.

*Bow your heads as the leader prays.*

All: **Amen.**

**A** **Work with Words**   Complete each sentence by unscrambling the words.

Jesus announced that God's (grien) _____ was at hand. By this he meant that God's reign of (eceap) _____, (vole) _____, and (itcejus) _____ had begun in him, but was still to come in its fullness. All Christians are (leldac) _____ by God to cooperate with him in bringing his kingdom to fullness. This calling from God is a (iaotvcno) _____. All who are baptized can serve their (rspaih) _____ in special ways. Ordained (iesprts) _____ and (eadcnos) _____ celebrate or assist at the sacraments and preach the word of God.

**B** **Check Understanding**   Complete the following: Every person is called . . .

_____

_____

## Activity    Live Your Faith

**Your Talents**   Draw the outline of your hand on a separate sheet of paper. On each finger, write one of your talents. Then in the center, write a way that you can use at least one of your talents to bring more peace and justice into the world.

# Family Faith

## ◎ Catholics Believe

■ Every person is called by God to a vocation.

■ Through your vocation, you can help God increase his reign.

## ✝ SCRIPTURE

Read *1 Corinthians 12:1–31* to learn more about the spiritual gifts with which God blesses us.

**GO ONLINE** www.harcourtreligion.com
For weekly Scripture readings and seasonal resources

## Activity

# Live Your Faith

**Name Acrostics** Sit and talk together. Discuss the gifts that you see in each member of your family. Then, using your names, create acrostics that list the gifts of your family. Here is an example:

J oyful
O thers come first
E nthusiastic

Discuss how your family members' gifts are making the world a better place.

# People of Faith

**Frederic** was born in Milan, Italy. For a time he studied law, but in Paris he discovered a great love for literature. He had a strong faith, and his friends challenged him to find a way to live out his Christian beliefs in his everyday life. Frederic cofounded the Society of Saint Vincent de Paul. This religious association continues today to help those in need, especially those who are poor. Blessed Frederic's feast day is September 8.

▲ **Blessed Frederic Ozanam**
**1813–1853**

## 🌷 Family Prayer

O God, help us answer your call as Blessed Frederic did, so that we may help you increase your reign of justice, love, and peace. Amen.

*In Unit 4 your child is learning about the CHURCH.*

# Chapter 11 Models of Faith

 Let Us Pray

**Leader:** Help us learn from those who serve you, O Lord.

"How good God is to the upright,
the LORD, to those who are clean of heart!"

*Psalm 73:1*

**All:** Help us learn from those who serve you, O Lord. Amen.

**Activity** Let's Begin

**I Believe** These quotations tell you about the personal beliefs of three famous people who helped change the world. Many who make a difference are as young as you are.

Now think about your beliefs.

• What statement about your own beliefs would you like people to remember?

"We must be the change we wish to see."
—*Mohandas Gandhi*

"You must do the thing you think you cannot do."
— *Eleanor Roosevelt*

"I cannot help it when I see injustice. I cannot keep quiet."
—*Archbishop Desmond Tutu*

**127**

# Holy Ones of God

 **Focus** What is faith?

The Church honors certain people whose whole lives showed others how to do God's will. These models of faith all helped God bring his reign into the world more fully. The Church calls each of these people a **saint**. Here are the stories of two of them.

### A BIOGRAPHY

# Catherine of Siena

Catherine wanted to serve God through quiet prayer. But Catherine's world was full of problems. God called her to make a difference.

Catherine lived long ago in Siena, Italy. She was very wise and used words well. Even though it was unusual for a woman of her time, Catherine made public speeches and taught priests. She also cared for those who were sick or in prison.

Catherine spoke out against injustice. She helped leaders in the Church make peace with one another. Christians learn from Catherine that every member of the Church can make a difference.

Catherine's students called her "Mother" and "Teacher." She has been named a Doctor of the Church.

## Holy Lives

Catherine of Siena is a canonized saint of the Catholic Church. This means that the Church has officially declared that she led a holy life and is enjoying eternal life with God in heaven.

❓ **What do you admire about Catherine?**

# Good Pope John

Words of Faith

A **saint** is a person who the Church declares has led a holy life and is enjoying eternal life with God in heaven.

Before he was elected pope, John XXIII served soldiers who were wounded in World War I. This experience taught him to work for peace. Later he worked with religious leaders who were not Catholic. He learned to look for things that were the same in their beliefs, rather than for differences.

After he was elected pope, John XXIII called all the world's bishops to Rome to renew and reform the Catholic Church at the Second Vatican Council. He died before it ended, but the council continued. People everywhere mourned the death of the humble, friendly man they called "Good Pope John." Pope John XXIII was named blessed by the Church in September 2000. This is the last step before a saint is canonized.

❓ **What quality of Pope John XXIII do you admire the most?**

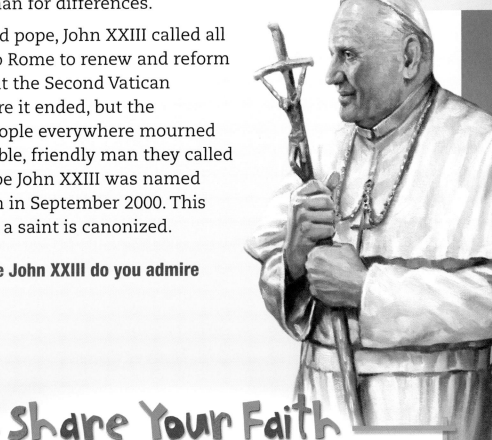

## Activity — Share Your Faith

**Reflect:** Think about what makes Saint Catherine and Pope John XXIII models of faith.

**Share:** Discuss your ideas about them with the class.

**Act:** Where the circles overlap, write what you know is true of both Saint Catherine and Pope John XXIII. In the circle on the left, write what is true only for Saint Catherine. Write what is true only for Pope John XXIII in the circle on the right.

Saint Catherine | Pope John XXIII

# Model of Holiness

◉ **Focus** How is Mary a model of holiness?

There are many saints, but Mary is the perfect model of holiness. God chose Mary to be the mother of Jesus. After Mary said "yes" to being the mother of God's Son, she visited her cousin Elizabeth. Here is how Mary described her joy at the great blessing God had given her.

✝ **SCRIPTURE**                                                    Luke 1: 46–50

## Mary's Song

"My soul proclaims the greatness of the Lord;
   my spirit rejoices in God my savior.
For he has looked upon his handmaid's lowliness;
   behold, from now on will all ages call
      me blessed.
The Mighty One has done great things for me,
   and holy is his name.
His mercy is from age to age
   to those who fear him."

*Luke 1:46–50*

God created Mary full of grace. He preserved her from sin from the very first moment of her conception. The Church calls this gift from God Mary's **Immaculate Conception**.

The word *immaculate* means spotless and clean—without sin. The word *conception* means the very moment when a person's life begins. The Catholic Church celebrates the Immaculate Conception of Mary on December 8.

❓ **Have you ever been given a very big responsibility? What did you say or do?**

130

*Madonna and Child* by Giambologna

## Your Will Be Done

Part of holiness is being able to accept and do the things that God asks of you. Mary accepted God's will throughout her life. Mary cared for and protected Jesus when he was a child. She stood by him all through his life. Mary was strong enough to be at the foot of Jesus' cross when he was crucified.

After Jesus ascended into heaven, Mary remained on earth with Jesus' followers. She was there at Pentecost when the Holy Spirit came to the disciples. Mary is called the Mother of the Church because she is an example of love and faith for Christians. Even today, she continues to hold all of her Son's followers close to her heart.

## A Guide for You

When you were baptized, you may have received the name of one of the saints of God. This person is your **patron saint**. He or she is your model of faith and prays for you from heaven. You walk in the footsteps of your saint and continue his or her good works in the way you live your life.

### Words of Faith

**Immaculate Conception** is the title for Mary that recognizes that God preserved her from sin from the first moment of her life.

A **patron saint** is a model of faith and a protector for you.

## Activity — Connect Your Faith

**Time for Holiness** Use the clock to show what you do each day. Divide the clock so that it looks like a sliced pie. You may have a narrow slice from seven o'clock to eight o'clock for getting up and preparing for school, but you may have a much larger slice for playing after school. After you have shown your activities for a day, color those that God's presence could make holy.

# Litany of the Saints

 Let Us Pray

*Gather and begin with the Sign of the Cross.*

**Leader:** Respond with **Pray for us** after each saint's name.

**Reader:** Holy Mary, Mother of God

**All:** **Pray for us.**

**Reader:** Saint Michael

Saint John the Baptist

Saint Joseph

Saints Peter and Paul

Saint Mary Magdalene

Saint Stephen

Saint Agnes

Saint Gregory

Saint Francis

Saint Dominic

Saint Catherine

Saint Teresa

Saints Perpetua and Felicity

Saint Martin

**Leader:** Let us pray.

*Bow your heads as the leader prays.*

**All:** **Amen.**

 *Sing together.*

We are God's people,
the flock of the Lord.

"Psalm 100" © 1969, 1981, 1997, ICEL.

# Review and Apply

**A** **Check Understanding**   Write responses on the lines below.

1. Name three ways that Catherine of Siena showed her holiness.

   _____

   _____

2. Why was Blessed John XXIII called Good Pope John?

   _____

3. What does it mean to be canonized?

   _____

4. What is meant by Mary's Immaculate Conception?

   _____

5. Why is Mary called the Mother of the Church?

   _____

**B** **Make Connections**   Name two ways that you can grow in holiness.

   _____

   _____

## Activity — Live Your Faith

**Saint Symbols**   Make a crest for a saint whom you admire. You may need to research more about him or her. On your crest, place a motto and symbols that show the qualities of the saint whom you will try to imitate.

# Family Faith

## ◎ Catholics Believe

■ The Church's holiness shines in the saints. All who live their love of God are saints.

■ Mary is the perfect model of holiness, and she is called the Mother of the Church.

### ✝ SCRIPTURE

Read *1 Thessalonians 4:13–15* for assurance that the saints are with God.

**GO ONLINE** www.harcourtreligion.com
For weekly Scripture readings and seasonal resources

## Activity

# Live Your Faith

**Scrapbook** Research a patron saint for your family. You can find information about many saints in your parish library or on the Internet. Also share stories about models of holiness in your own family. Create a scrapbook with drawings and descriptions of all the models of faith you find.

Priest Honored

Models of Holiness

# People of Faith

▲ **Blessed Kateri Tekakwitha**
1656–1680

**Kateri Tekakwitha** is the first Native American to be nearing canonization. She was the daughter of a Mohawk warrior and an Algonquian woman who was Christian. Kateri was born in New York in 1656 and was baptized in 1676. She devoted herself to a life of prayer, penance, and the care of those who were sick or old. After her First Communion in 1677, Kateri's devotion to the Eucharist strengthened her faith. She was named Blessed in 1980. Her feast day is April 17.

##  Family Prayer

O God, help us grow in holiness as Kateri did. Help us imitate her love for you and her devotion to the Eucharist. Amen.

*In Unit 4 your child is learning about the CHURCH.*

# Chapter 12
# The Church Teaches

## Let Us Pray

**Leader:** God, help us follow in your faithful ways.

"Send your light and fidelity,
  that they may be my guide."
*Psalm 43:3*

**All:** God, help us follow in your faithful ways.
Amen.

## Activity — Let's Begin

### A Good Teacher Is . . .

- someone who encourages you to think but allows you to learn from mistakes.

- someone who cares about who you are and what you learn.

- someone who isn't afraid to smile or cry.

- What other statements would you add about good teachers?

# Jesus Chooses a Teacher

 **Focus** How did Jesus choose Peter as the leader of the Apostles?

The Church is your most important teacher. The Church's authority, or power to teach, was given by Jesus and is guided by the Holy Spirit. Here is a Gospel story about the beginnings of the Church's authority to teach.

✝ S C R I P T U R E                                    Mark 8:27–30

## You Are the Messiah!

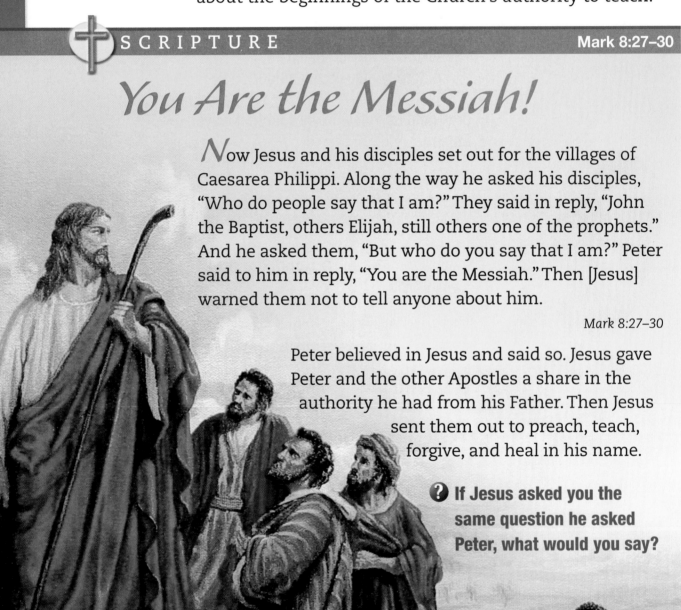

*N*ow Jesus and his disciples set out for the villages of Caesarea Philippi. Along the way he asked his disciples, "Who do people say that I am?" They said in reply, "John the Baptist, others Elijah, still others one of the prophets." And he asked them, "But who do you say that I am?" Peter said to him in reply, "You are the Messiah." Then [Jesus] warned them not to tell anyone about him.

*Mark 8:27–30*

Peter believed in Jesus and said so. Jesus gave Peter and the other Apostles a share in the authority he had from his Father. Then Jesus sent them out to preach, teach, forgive, and heal in his name.

❓ **If Jesus asked you the same question he asked Peter, what would you say?**

© Harcourt Religion

136

## Peter Denies Jesus

Peter made some mistakes along the way. Much later, at the time of Jesus' crucifixion, Peter and the other disciples were very much afraid. In fact, the night before Jesus died, Peter denied three times that he had ever known Jesus. Afterward, he was ashamed of himself and cried bitterly.

## Feed My Lambs

But Jesus never lost faith in Peter. After Jesus' death and Resurrection, Jesus was talking to Peter and the other disciples on the shore of a lake. Jesus asked three times whether Peter loved him. Of course, Peter said that he did. Jesus said to him, "Feed my lambs. Feed my sheep." See *John 21:15–17.*

In spite of Peter's earlier denials, Jesus made Peter the chief shepherd of all his flock. When he became the leader, Peter made good decisions for the members of the Church.

❓ **Why do you think Jesus asked Peter the same question three times?**

**Activity** — Share Your Faith

**Reflect:** Think of some times when you have been forgiven for mistakes you have made.

**Share:** During a short class prayer, mention the name of someone who has forgiven you.

**Act:** Using a separate sheet of paper, show a situation in which someone in authority gave you a second chance.

© Harcourt Religion

# The Church and You

 **Focus** What is your role as a member of the Church?

After Jesus ascended into heaven, Peter and all the disciples were afraid. Then on Pentecost, the Holy Spirit came and gave them courage. They went out and began to preach the good news.

The Apostles, with Peter as their head, were the first leaders of the Church. Jesus founded the Church on the Apostles. He gave them the authority to teach and lead his followers. Today the chief teachers in the Church are the pope and the bishops, the successors of the Apostles. Their authority to teach, called the **magisterium**, goes back to the authority Christ first gave to the Apostles. The Holy Spirit works through the Church's teachers to keep the whole Church faithful to the teachings of Jesus.

## Your Role

The Church's mission to share the true message of Jesus is not left to the pope and bishops alone. All members of the Body of Christ have a duty to learn Jesus' message as the Church interprets it and to share it with others. As you do this, you will grow in your love of God and neighbor.

 **❓ Who has taught you what the Church teaches?**

© Harcourt Religion

138

# Rules for Living

Some of the responsibilities of members of the Catholic Church are summed up in the **precepts of the Church**. The Church's leaders developed these rules to show you the minimum you should do to live morally and faithfully. As a Catholic, you have a duty to live according to the teachings and precepts of the Church.

## Precepts of the Church

1. Take part in the Mass on Sundays and holy days. Keep these days holy and avoid unnecessary work.

2. Celebrate the Sacrament of Reconciliation at least once a year if you have committed a serious sin.

3. Receive Holy Communion at least once a year during Easter time.

4. Observe days of fasting and abstinence.

5. Give your time, gifts, and money to support the Church.

## Words of Faith

The **magisterium** is the Church's teaching authority to interpret the word of God found in Scripture and Tradition.

The **precepts of the Church** are some of the minimum requirements given by Church leaders for deepening your relationship with God and the Church.

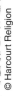

## Activity — Connect Your Faith

**Word Search**   Find at least six words in this word search puzzle that relate to the teaching authority of the Church.

| F | A | I | T | H | O | P | E | A | P |
|---|---|---|---|---|---|---|---|---|---|
| B | P | R | E | C | E | P | T | S | E |
| H | O | L | Y | S | P | I | R | I | T |
| A | P | O | S | T | L | E | S | C | E |
| D | E | B | I | S | H | O | P | S | R |

Use three of these words in a sentence about your role in the Church.

_____

_____

© Harcourt Religion

# Prayer to the Holy Spirit

 Let Us Pray

*Gather and begin with the Sign of the Cross.*

*Sing together the refrain.*

Come Lord Jesus,
send us your Spirit,
renew the face of the earth.
Come Lord Jesus,
send us your Spirit,
renew the face of the earth.

"Send Us Your Spirit" © 1981, 1982, 1987, GIA Publications, Inc.

*The Pentecost* by Juan de Juanes

**Group 1:** Come, Holy Spirit, fill the hearts of your faithful. And kindle in them the fire of your love.

**All:** *Sing refrain.*

**Group 2:** Send forth your Spirit and they shall be created. And you shall renew the face of the earth.

**All:** *Sing refrain.*

**Lord, by the light of the Holy Spirit you have taught the hearts of your faithful. In the same Spirit, help us desire what is right and always rejoice in your consolation. We ask this through Christ our Lord. Amen.**

**Leader:** Let us pray.

*Bow your heads as the leader prays.*

**All:** **Amen.**

# Review and Apply

**A** **Work with Words**   Complete each sentence with the correct term from the Word Bank.

**WORD BANK**

precepts
Holy Spirit
authority
live
  according to
Church
magisterium

1.  Some of the rules that the Church gives to help you grow closer to Jesus are called the _____ of the Church.

2.  Jesus gave the Church the _____ to teach and lead the Body of Christ.

3.  You have the duty to _____ the rules and laws of the Church.

4.  The _____ is the teaching authority of the Church.

5.  The Church and the magisterium are guided by the _____.

**B** **Check Understanding**   List two of the precepts of the Church. How do they help you become a better member of the Church?

_____

_____

_____

**Activity**   Live Your Faith

**More About Peter**   Find in the Bible the story of Peter's denial of Jesus *(Mark 14:66–72)* and the story of Jesus and Peter as they talked on the shore *(John 21:1–19)*. Think of a creative way to retell one of these stories—a radio play, a song, or a skit. Perform your story for the class.

# Family Faith

## Catholics Believe

- Jesus gave the leaders of the Church the authority to interpret Scripture and Tradition for the faithful.

- The Holy Spirit directs the Church in teaching and guiding the People of God.

### ✝ SCRIPTURE

Read *Nehemiah 8:1–12* to see how the ancient Israelites kept the Sabbath.

 **www.harcourtreligion.com**
For weekly Scripture readings and seasonal resources

## Activity

# Live Your Faith

**Sunday Suggestions**   As a family, choose ways to observe the Church precept to keep Sunday holy. Create a list of *dos* and *don'ts*. For example:

- **Do** go to Mass.
- **Do** visit relatives.
- **Do** have a family picnic.
- **Don't** spend the day shopping at the mall.
- **Don't** make sports more important than God

Encourage one another to practice these suggestions on the next Sunday. Discuss the experience.

# People of Faith

▲ **Saint Mary Magdalen Postel 1756–1846**

**Mary Magdalen Postel** was educated in a Benedictine convent, where she dedicated herself to God. At eighteen she opened a school for girls in France just before the French Revolution broke out. During the revolution her school was closed, and Mary Magdalen became a leader who sheltered fugitive priests. After the revolution Mary Magdalen Postel continued to work in the field of religious education. Her teachings became well known. Saint Mary Magdalen's feast day is July 16.

## Family Prayer

Saint Mary Magdalen, pray for us that we may open our hearts and minds to learn more as we grow in faith and in our love for God. Amen.

*In Unit 4 your child is learning about the CHURCH.*

**A** **Work with Words**   Solve the puzzle with terms from the Word Bank.

| WORD BANK | | | |
|---|---|---|---|
| vocation | canonization | kingdom | laity |
| conception | saint | patron saint | |
| magisterium | precepts | altar server | |

## Down

1. A _____ is God's call to serve him and others.

2. God's _____ is here now, but has not yet come in its fullness.

3. Observing days of fasting and abstinence is one of the _____ of the Church.

4. The Church's teaching authority to interpret Scripture and Tradition

6. The Immaculate _____ is the teaching that Mary was preserved from sin from the first moment of her life.

7. A person who the Church declares has lead a holy life and is enjoying life with God in heaven

## Across

5. Assists the priest at Mass

8. The process by which the Church officially declares someone a saint

9. A model of faith and a protector for you

10. All the baptized who are not priests or religious brothers or sisters

# UNIT 5
## Faithful Living

**Chapter 13 Family Love**

*What do the commandments teach about family love?*

**Chapter 14 Choosing Life**

*Why is all human life sacred?*

**Chapter 15 Live in Truth**

*Why is it important to be truthful?*

 What do you think you will learn in this unit about faithful living?

# Chapter 13 Family Love

## Let Us Pray

**Leader:** God, may we always share your happiness with those we love.

"Happy are all who fear the LORD, who walk in the ways of God."

*Psalm 128:1*

**All:** God, may we always share your happiness with those we love. Amen.

## Activity — Let's Begin

**All Shapes and Sizes** God loves each family, no matter what its shape or size. He wants each family member to be a sign of his love within the family.

• Who in your family has shown you God's love?

# Families in God's Plan

 **Focus** What makes families strong?

God's plan for humans includes living in families. The following story shares an important lesson about living as a family.

## A FABLE

# The Bundle of Sticks

Some brothers and sisters were quarreling among themselves, so their father asked them to bring him a handful of sticks. He tied the sticks together in a bundle. Then the father placed the bundle in the hands of each child in turn and said, "Break it into pieces." None of the children could break the bundle.

Then the father separated the sticks and handed one to each child. The children broke the individual sticks easily. Their father told them, "If you are divided among yourselves, you will be broken as easily as these individual sticks. But if you unite to help one another, you will be strong, like the bundle of sticks. You will not be overcome by attempts to divide you."

Based on an Aesop fable

 **What is the lesson of this fable? Name a time when your family has learned the same lesson.**

146

# Family Unity

God created humans to live in families. Like the father in the story, God wants families to be strong, to protect one another, and to live in peace and love.

The fourth, sixth, and ninth commandments provide basic laws about family love and respect. The fourth commandment is this: Honor your father and mother. Jesus is the perfect example for living out this commandment.

## ✝ SCRIPTURE          Luke 2:41–52

# Jesus and His Family

When Jesus was twelve, he went to Jerusalem with his family to celebrate Passover. As Mary and Joseph were returning home, they realized that Jesus was not with them. They finally found him talking with the teachers in the Temple. Mary told Jesus how worried they had been, and Jesus returned to Nazareth with his parents.

Jesus was obedient as he grew in wisdom and age. His actions were pleasing to God and to all who knew him.

Based on *Luke 2:41–52*

❓ **Why is it important to obey your parents?**

## Activity  Share Your Faith

**Reflect:** What keeps a family strong and close?

**Share:** Talk about these things in a group.

**Act:** Imagine that your group is working on a new TV series about families. Come up with a name for the series and titles for three episodes.

# Commandments for Families

**Focus** What do the commandments teach about family love?

The fourth commandment teaches you to honor your parents and guardians. You honor them when you

- listen to and **obey** them in all that is good.
- show gratitude for all that they do for you.
- respect and care for them as they grow older.
- respect people in authority.

Parents and guardians provide for your needs, serve as good role models, and share their faith with you. They help you grow in faith, make good choices, and decide your vocation.

## Faithful Love

The sixth commandment is this: You shall not commit adultery. The ninth is this: You shall not covet your neighbor's wife. These commandments are about the faithful love and commitment between married couples.

When a man and woman marry, they make solemn promises called **vows**. They promise to love and honor each other always and to welcome the gift of children.

Part of being faithful is respecting the vows of other married couples and not acting in ways that could weaken their marriage. Adultery means being unfaithful to these vows. The grace of the Sacrament of Matrimony strengthens the couple to be faithful and true.

❓ **What does it mean to be a good role model? Who has been a good role model for you?**

## Faith Fact

About 260,000 Catholic marriages are celebrated each year in the United States.

© Harcourt Religion

**148**

## Faithfulness and You

The sixth and ninth commandments apply to everyone. You can live out these commandments by keeping promises to family, friends, and God. You can practice **modesty** by dressing, talking, and acting in ways that honor your own dignity and that of others. You can respect that the differences between males and females are gifts from God.

## Family Disappointments

Sometimes it is hard for families to live as God intends. Arguments, hurts, and disappointments can keep families from being signs of God's love. Parents and children sometimes hurt one another. Some families are hurt through separation, divorce, or even death.

But God continues to love all families and to help them grow stronger. Every time families are signs of love, they reflect the love that exists within the Holy Trinity.

❓ **What can families do to be signs of God's love?**

© Harcourt Religion

## Words of Faith

To **obey** is to do things or act in certain ways that are requested by those in authority.

**Vows** are solemn promises that are made to or before God.

**Modesty** is the virtue that helps people dress, talk, and act in appropriate ways.

**Activity** Connect Your Faith

**Build with Solid Blocks** The family is the building block of the Christian community and of society. In the blocks, write at least six qualities of good friendships and family love. Tell how your family shows one of these qualities to others.

# Prayer of Petition

 Let Us Pray

*Gather and begin with the Sign of the Cross.*

**Leader:** God, from you every family learns to love. We ask you to strengthen our families.

**All:** **Hear us, O Lord.**

**Reader 1:** May parents and those who care for us be blessed in their commitment to love their children and each other.

**All:** **Hear us, O Lord.**

**Reader 2:** May all children find support and security in their families.

**All:** **Hear us, O Lord.**

**Reader 3:** May all families discover your gift of faithful love.

**All:** **Hear us, O Lord.**

**Leader:** Let us pray.

*Bow your heads as the leader prays.*

**All:** **Amen.**

 *Sing together.*

All grownups, all children,
all mothers, all fathers
are sisters and brothers
in the fam'ly of God.

"All Grownups, All Children"
© 2000, GIA Publications, Inc.

Harcourt Religion

**150**

**A** **Work with Words**   Complete each sentence with the correct term from the Word Bank.

God made humans to live as

_____ who love and
respect one another. By following the

_____ commandment,

children _____ and
obey their parents and guardians. The

_____ and ninth commandments are

about being _____
in marriage, keeping promises, and practicing

_____.

| WORD BANK |
| --- |
| faithful |
| modesty |
| fourth |
| families |
| sixth |
| honor |

**B** **Make Connections**   Write three ways you will follow the fourth commandment this week.

_____

_____

_____

## Activity   Live Your Faith

**Be Positive**   Write three bumper sticker slogans that can help families live the fourth, sixth, and ninth commandments. Think of positive phrases to help people remember what to do.

# Family Faith

## ◎ Catholics Believe

- God created humans to live in strong, loving families.

- The fourth, sixth, and ninth commandments provide basic laws of family love and respect.

### ✝ SCRIPTURE

Read *Galatians 6:9–10* to find out about love in the family of faith.

GO
ONLINE
**www.harcourtreligion.com**
For weekly Scripture readings and seasonal resources

## Activity
# Live Your Faith

**Make Coupons** Discuss with your family something you shared with your class this week. Then talk about the importance of showing love to one another. Make coupons that can be given to family members at appropriate times.

Example:

~ COUPON ~
Good for one hug.

---

▲ Saints Anne and Joachim
first century B.C.

# People of Faith

Little is known about the parents of Mary. Legend says that **Anne** and **Joachim** had wanted a child for a long time. When Mary was born, they took her to the Temple and dedicated her to God. Anne and Joachim raised Mary to respect others, to be faithful to God, and to follow God's ways in all things. Saint Anne is the patron of women who are childless and women who are pregnant. Saint Anne is often pictured teaching Mary to read. The feast day of Saints Anne and Joachim is July 26.

## ✿ Family Prayer

Saints Anne and Joachim, pray for our families, that we may become signs of God's loving and forgiving presence to one another and to the world. Amen.

*In Unit 5 your child is learning about MORALITY.*

# Chapter 14 Choosing Life

## Let Us Pray

**Leader:** God, we thank you for your precious gifts of life and light.

"For with you is the fountain of life,
and in your light we see light."
*Psalm 36:10*

**All:** God, we thank you for your precious gifts of life and light. Amen.

## Activity Let's Begin

### If I Can Stop One Heart from Breaking

If I can stop one heart from breaking,
I shall not live in vain;
If I can ease one life the aching,
Or cool one pain,
Or help one fainting robin
Unto his nest again,
I shall not live in vain.

Emily Dickinson

• What are your thoughts about making your life worthwhile?

Explore

# Respect Life

**◉ Focus** How do you respect life?

Living a worthwhile life means respecting and caring for others' lives. Here is a true story about a man who made a choice to respect life.

BIOGRAPHY

## A CHANGE OF HEART

About eighty years ago Alfred Nobel picked up the morning paper and, to his horror, read his own death notice! The newspaper had reported his death by mistake. Nobel read the bold heading, "Dynamite King Dies." In the article he was described as a merchant of death.

Nobel was saddened. Although he had made a fortune by inventing dynamite, he did not want to be remembered as a "merchant of death." From then on, he devoted his energy and money to works of peace and the good of humankind.

Today, Alfred Nobel is remembered as the founder of the Nobel Prizes, especially the Peace Prize. These prizes reward and encourage people who work for the good of others.

**❓ If your death notice were written accidentally today, what could it say about your respect for the lives of others?**

Nobel Peace Prize winners

154

# The Fifth Commandment

Alfred Nobel changed the direction of his life and began supporting work that gave life to others. He was a clear example of respect for the fifth commandment: You shall not kill.

All human life is sacred, and all actions that support and protect life support the fifth commandment. At the end of his life Moses told the people to remember that God's law was life for them.

✝ SCRIPTURE

I call heaven and earth today to witness against you: I have set before you life and death, the blessing and the curse. Choose life, then, that you and your descendants may live, by loving the LORD, your God, heeding his voice, and holding fast to him. For that will mean life for you. . . .

*Deuteronomy 30:19–20*

## A Path to Life

God's laws show the path to life and happiness. The fifth commandment reminds you of the fundamental respect for life that is owed to every person. Because every life comes from God, every human life is sacred from the moment of conception until the time of death.

**Activity** — Share Your Faith

**Reflect:** Think about someone you know who deserves a prize for the way that he or she respects life.

**Share:** Share with a partner what this person does to respect life.

**Act:** Design a medal to honor the person you chose. Write his or her name on the line.

_____

# Keeping the Fifth Commandment

 **Focus** How do you keep the fifth commandment?

All human life is sacred, including the life of the unborn and the elderly. The life of an unborn child is most fragile, and it is deserving of the greatest respect and care. Thus, the intentional ending of the life of an unborn child is a grave sin.

The taking of one's own life is suicide. It is seriously contrary to God's gift of life and love. However, one's responsibility may be lessened by mental illness. **Murder**, the intentional killing of an innocent person, is seriously sinful because it contradicts Jesus' law of love. To kill in self-defense, however, is justified, if it is the only way to protect one's own life.

The Catholic Church teaches that the death penalty, or capital punishment, is almost always wrong. Alternatives, such as life in prison without parole, are preferred.

## Respect for the Body

The Church teaches that your body and soul are united. You are a temple in which God's Spirit dwells. The fifth commandment teaches you to respect your body and those of others. Eating healthful foods and getting enough exercise are important to protect your life and health. At your age, using alcohol is an offense against the fifth commandment. The use of tobacco and illegal drugs is harmful to the body. Tempting or encouraging others to disrespect the gift of life is wrong, too.

❓ **What can you do to help others respect life?**

© Harcourt Religion

## Jesus' Message

Jesus said that even anger can be sinful if it is not controlled; anger can harden into hatred. Hatred can lead to revenge, or getting back at someone for something that has happened, or to violence.

It can be difficult to show love and respect for those who bully or treat you unfairly. Jesus calls you to love in this way.

## Words of Faith

**Murder** is the intentional killing of an innocent person.

### ✝ SCRIPTURE                    Matthew 5:43–45

## Love of Enemies

You have heard that it was said, "You shall love your neighbor and hate your enemy." But I say to you, love your enemies, and pray for those who persecute you, that you may be children of your heavenly Father, for he makes his sun rise on the bad and the good, and causes rain to fall on the just and unjust.

*Matthew 5:43–45*

❓ **What did Jesus mean when he said that God makes his sun rise on the bad and the good?**

## Activity — Connect Your Faith

**Choose Life**   Circle one life-giving action that you will practice today.

- Protect unborn children.
- Let go of anger.
- Forgive your enemies.
- Set a good example for others.
- Show respect for your body by eating healthful foods.

# Celebration of the Word

**Let Us Pray**

*Gather and begin with the Sign of the Cross.*

**Reader 1:** A reading from the First Letter of Peter.

*Read 1 Peter 3:9–12.*

The word of the Lord.

**All:** **Thanks be to God.**

**Reader 2:** When we are given the choice to walk away or to stay and fight,

**All:** **Help us choose your way, O Lord.**

**Reader 3:** When we are given the choice to stay angry or to forgive,

**All:** **Help us choose your way, O Lord.**

**Reader 4:** When we are given the chance to help those who are sick, disabled, or elderly,

**All:** **Help us choose your way, O Lord.**

**Leader:** Let us pray.

*Bow your heads as the leader prays.*

**All:** **Amen.**

*Sing together.*

Jesu, Jesu, fill us with your love, show us how to serve the neighbors we have from you.

"Jesu, Jesu." © 1969, Hope Publishing Co.

Celebrate

# Review and Apply

**A** **Check Understanding** Complete the following statements.

1. The fifth commandment says this:

   _____ .

2. One way you can follow the fifth commandment is by

   _____ .

3. One serious sin against the fifth commandment is

   _____ .

4. All human life is _____ .

5. Hatred can lead to _____ .

**B** **Make Connections** Write brief answers to these questions.
What new lesson did Jesus give about the fifth
commandment?

_____ .

How do you show that you respect life?

_____ .

## Activity Live Your Faith

**Brainstorm** What are three
steps you can take to control
your anger when you are in a
difficult situation? Write them
here.

# Family Faith

## ◎ Catholics Believe

- All human life is sacred because it comes from God.

- The fifth commandment forbids anything that takes a human life.

### ✝ SCRIPTURE

Read *Isaiah 9:1–6* to find out about the Prince of Peace.

**www.harcourtreligion.com**
For weekly Scripture readings and seasonal resources

## Activity

# Live Your Faith

**Write a Letter of Thanks**  Research the life and work of a recent Nobel Peace Prize winner who is still alive. Find out about the person's contribution and how he or she has worked for peace. Write a letter to the person, thanking him or her for choosing life.

# People of Faith

▲ Saint Maximilian Kolbe
1894–1941

**Maximilian Kolbe** was ordained a Franciscan priest and was devoted to Our Lady of the Immaculate Conception. During World War II he was imprisoned at Auschwitz. While in prison, Maximilian encouraged other prisoners to hold fast to God's love. He volunteered to take the place of a young father condemned to execution by the Nazis. He chose life even as he gave his own for another. Maximilian was named a saint in 1982. His feast day is August 14.

##  Family Prayer

Saint Maximilian Kolbe, pray for us that we may be faithful to God's love and always choose the path of life and hope. Amen.

© Harcourt Religion

*In Unit 5 your child is learning about MORALITY.*

# Chapter 15 Live in Truth

 **Let Us Pray**

**Leader:** Lord God, may we always be honest in our praise of you.

"Teach me, LORD, your way
that I may walk in your truth,"

*Psalm 86:11*

**All:** Lord God, may we always be honest in our praise of you.
Amen.

Honesty is the best policy.

I cannot tell a lie.

The truth will set you free.

**Activity** Let's Begin

**It's the Truth!** Look at the sayings on the board.

• Create your own saying about the importance of telling the truth.

161

# Honest Choices

 **Focus** How do people witness to the truth?

Thomas More, an important official in England in the sixteenth century, was imprisoned for refusing to tell a lie. Thomas had an important decision to make. In a letter to his daughter, he discussed his dilemma.

## A LETTER

## THOMAS MORE

My dearest Meg,

Your father greets you with all his affection but not much hope. The dilemma I face will not soon go away.

I have been imprisoned now for some months. All I have to do to be set free is to take the Oath of Supremacy. But how can I?

If I take the oath, I will be saying that Henry VIII is the supreme head of the Catholic Church in England. You know that my Catholic faith is strong, and I believe that the pope is the true head of the Catholic Church.

King Henry is angry. He is afraid that if I go against him, other people will follow my example. I am being forced to make a choice: be honest and be killed, or tell a lie and live.

Pray for me.
Your loving father,

Thomas More

❓ **Have you ever had to decide whether to speak the truth, tell a lie, or remain silent? What happened?**

## Living the Truth

Thomas More chose to remain true to his beliefs and speak the truth. As a result, the king had him killed, but the Catholic Church named him a saint. Many saints and heroes have suffered torture and death for the sake of the truth of their faith. A person who stays faithful to Christ and suffers and dies rather than denying the truth is called a **martyr**. Martyrs live the truth by backing up their words with actions.

You probably will not be called on to be a martyr. But every follower of Jesus is called to live in the truth. By your actions you show your faithfulness to Jesus and the truth of his message.

## Words of Faith

A **martyr** is someone who gives up his or her life to witness to the truth of the faith.

### Activity

## Share Your Faith

**Truth-telling**

**Reflect:** Think about why it is always best to tell the truth.

**Share:** With a partner, list ten reasons for truth-telling.

**Act:** List words for a song about truth-telling.

_____   _____   _____

# The Eighth Commandment

 **Focus** What does the eighth commandment call you to do?

God is the source of all truth. His word and his law call people to live in the truth. The eighth commandment says this: You shall not bear false witness against your neighbor.

The eighth commandment forbids lying, or purposely not telling the truth. Lying can take many forms. If a person lies in court when under oath, he or she commits perjury, or false witness. Gossip is talking about another person behind his or her back. Gossip may or may not be a lie, but all gossip can harm the good reputation of another person.

All lies are unjust and unloving. All require **reparation**, or repair. Reparation may be as simple as an apology, or it may take more work, such as trying to help a person get back the reputation you have hurt.

❷ **What are some ways you can repair the damage to another person when you have not told the truth?**

# Jesus Is the Truth

Living in the spirit of the eighth commandment is more than not lying. You must choose to be truthful in words and actions. When you are truthful, you are living as a follower of Jesus, who always told the truth.

## ✝ SCRIPTURE                    John 8:31–32, 14:6

### The Truth Will Set You Free

Jesus . . . said . . . , "If you remain in my word, you will truly be my disciples, and you will know the truth, and the truth will set you free. . . . I am the way and the truth and the life. No one comes to the Father except through me."

*John 8:31–32, 14:6*

People trusted what Jesus did and said. When you are truthful, people trust you. When you promise to tell the truth, you have a special duty. Let your "yes" mean "yes" and your "no" mean "no." Telling the truth will set you free to follow Jesus and to live in love.

## Words of Faith

**Reparation** is action taken to repair the damage done by sin.

## Activity — Connect Your Faith

**Live the Truth**   Read the following list, and mark an X if a statement talks about living in truth and an O if it does not. For each statement marked with an O, tell one way the person could make up for his or her wrong choice.

_____ Juanita heard an unkind story about a classmate. She did not repeat it.

_____ Scott bragged falsely about how good he was at sports.

_____ Samantha told her parents that she was going to the library, but instead she went to the park.

_____ Maria discovered that her friend had shoplifted. She did not tell her other friends.

© Harcourt Religion

**165**

# Prayer of Petition

 Let Us Pray

*Gather and begin with the Sign of the Cross.*

**Leader:** Whenever we are afraid to tell the truth,

**All:** **Spirit of Truth, guide us!**

**Leader:** Whenever we are tempted to gossip,

**All:** **Spirit of Truth, guide us!**

**Leader:** Whenever we are faced with choices about telling the truth,

**All:** **Spirit of Truth, guide us!**

**Leader:** Whenever we falsely judge another,

**All:** **Spirit of Truth, guide us!**

**Leader:** God of all truth, whenever we face choices about telling the truth, guide us to your light. Give us strength to make good choices. We ask this in Jesus' name. Amen.

*Sing together.*

Send down the fire of your justice, Send down the rains of your love; Come, send down the Spirit, breathe life in your people, and we shall be people of God.

"Send Down the Fire" ©2001, GIA Publications, Inc.

# Review and Apply

**A** **Check Understanding** Circle True if a statement is true, and circle False if a statement is false. Correct any false statements.

1. A martyr is someone who gives up his or her life to witness to Jesus and the truth of the faith.

   True        False _____

2. Three sins against the eighth commandment are false witness, perjury, and love.

   True        False _____

3. Reparation is repairing a wrong.

   True        False _____

4. The eighth commandment is "You shall not kill."

   True        False _____

5. Only martyrs are called to live in truth.

   True        False _____

**B** **Make Connections** Write a response on the lines below. What did Jesus mean when he said, "The truth will set you free"?

_____

_____

## Activity — Live Your Faith

**Mini-dramas** Work with a group.

- Create a skit in which a person hurts another or damages another's reputation by telling a lie.

- Show how the person makes reparation for the wrong that he or she has done.

# Family Faith

## ◉ Catholics Believe

■ Because God is truth, his people are called to live in the truth.

■ The eighth commandment forbids lying.

### ✝ SCRIPTURE

Read *Proverbs 12:12–26* to learn more about the rewards that await those who are honest.

**GO** **ONLINE** **www.harcourtreligion.com**
For weekly Scripture readings and seasonal resources

## Activity

# Live Your Faith

**Truth Talk** As a family, take time this week to talk about the following questions:
- How do you handle a situation in which being honest would hurt someone?
- When is it right to tell on someone, and when is it wrong?
- How can you help one another live in truth?

# People of Faith

Joan of Arc was true to God's will and truth. She had visions and heard voices that told her to lead an army to fight for truth and save France from invaders. She bravely told the truth about her visions and voices and saved France in many battles. However, Joan was accused of being against the Church and of being a witch. She was burned at the stake when she was still a teenager. Joan was named a saint in 1920, and her feast day is May 30.

▲ Saint Joan of Arc 1412–1431

## 🌷 Family Prayer

Saint Joan of Arc, pray for us that we may grow strong in our faith and have the courage to speak and live the truth. Amen.

© Harcourt Religion

*In Unit 5 your child is learning about* MORALITY.

  See *Catechism of the Catholic Church* 1741, 2465–2470 *for further reading on chapter content.*

**A** **Work with Words**   Use the clues to solve the puzzle.

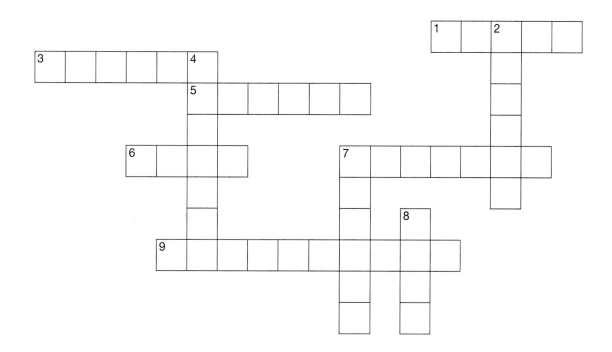

## Across

**1.** This commandment says: You shall not kill.

**3.** The intentional killing of an innocent person

**5.** This commandment says: You shall not bear false witness against your neighbor.

**6.** To do things or act in certain ways that are requested by those in authority

**7.** The virtue that helps people dress, talk, and act in appropriate ways

**9.** Action taken to repair the damage done through sin

## Down

**2.** This commandment specifically addresses sons and daughters.

**4.** Continuing the cycle of anger and hatred

**7.** Someone who gives up his or her life to witness to the truth of the faith

**8.** Solemn promises that are made to or before God

# UNIT 6
## The Paschal Mystery

**Chapter 16**

# The Church Year

*What does the Church year celebrate?*

**Chapter 17**

# The Seven Sacraments

*How do the sacraments help you grow?*

**Chapter 18**

# Healing and Reconciliation

*What is Jesus' message of forgiveness?*

**What do you think you will learn in this unit about the Paschal mystery?**

# Chapter 16 The Church Year

**Let Us Pray**

**Leader:** Creator God, we rejoice in the beauty and variety of your creation.

"The heavens declare the glory of God; the sky proclaims its builder's craft."

*Psalm 19:2*

**All:** Creator God, we rejoice in the beauty and variety of your creation. Amen.

**Activity** Let's Begin

**The Life Cycle** All living things follow a pattern. They come to life, they grow and develop, and finally they die. This pattern is called a life cycle. Every year as the seasons change, you see changes in the world around you. The change of seasons affects you, too.

• Tell about one seasonal change that happens where you live.

© Harcourt Religion

**171**

# The Cycle of Life

 **Focus** What is the Paschal mystery?

Your life is full of cycles and seasons. As you grow in faith, you will notice them more. A wise man once wrote a poem about the cycle of life. It is in the Bible.

## ✝ SCRIPTURE                          Ecclesiastes 3:1–8

## The Right Time

There is an appointed time for everything,
and a time for every affair under the heavens.

A time to be born, and a time to die;
   a time to plant, and a time to uproot the plant.

A time to kill, and a time to heal;
   a time to tear down, and a time to build.

A time to weep, and a time to laugh;
   a time to mourn, and a time to dance.

A time to scatter stones, and a time to
      gather them;
   a time to embrace, and a time to be far
      from embraces.

A time to seek, and a time to lose;
   a time to keep, and a time to cast away.

A time to rend, and a time to sew;
   a time to be silent, and a time
      to speak.

A time to love, and a time to hate;
   a time of war, and a time of peace.

*Ecclesiastes 3:1–8*

❓ **What do you think the poet wants you to understand?**

## The Paschal Mystery

Jesus experienced the natural cycle of life, but his life cycle did not end with his death on the cross. God the Father raised Jesus from the dead. Then Jesus ascended to join his Father in heaven. The suffering, death, Resurrection, and Ascension of Jesus are called the Paschal mystery . This mystery reveals that Jesus saved all humans from the power of sin and everlasting death.

The Church celebrates this mystery in every sacrament and especially at every Eucharist. Every Sunday you gather with the parish community to celebrate the new life that Jesus' Resurrection gives you.

## The Liturgical Year

From week to week at Sunday Mass, you may notice different readings, hymns, and colors. These mark the seasons of the Church's year, called the liturgical year . The liturgical year begins on the first Sunday of Advent, usually around December 1, and ends with the feast of Christ the King.

❷ **What signs of the present liturgical season do you see?**

© Harcourt Religion

### Words of Faith

The **Paschal mystery** is the mystery of Jesus' suffering, death, Resurrection, and Ascension.

The **liturgical year** is the cycle of feasts and seasons that make up the Church's year of worship.

---

### Activity — Share Your Faith

**Reflect:** Reflect on the things you did last week.

**Share:** With a partner, share some of the best times and worst times you had last week.

**Act:** In the boxes below, sketch a symbol for the "times" of your life. If Monday was a happy time, draw a symbol to show that you were happy. Use different symbols to represent your "times."

| SUNDAY | MONDAY | TUESDAY | WEDNESDAY | THURSDAY | FRIDAY | SATURDAY |
|--------|--------|---------|-----------|----------|--------|----------|
|        |        |         |           |          |        |          |

# The Seasons

 **Focus** What are the seasons of the Church year?

Just as the seasons of the year mark the cycles of life and death in nature, the seasons of the liturgical year mark and celebrate the events of the Paschal mystery.

Advent

Christmas

Ordinary Time

Ordinary Time

Easter

Triduum

Lent

## Advent

Advent is the beginning of the Church year. The four weeks before Christmas are a time of preparation for the coming of Jesus. The Church asks the Holy Spirit to help people welcome Jesus into their hearts every day. The seasonal color is violet, a sign of waiting.

## Christmas

The Christmas Season lasts from Christmas Eve through the Sunday after Epiphany, which is twelve days after Christmas. It is a time to be joyful and to thank God the Father for sending his Son to become one of us. White and gold colors are reminders to celebrate the gift of Jesus.

**❓ How do your family and parish prepare for Christmas?**

## Lent

Lent lasts for forty days. It begins on Ash Wednesday and ends on Holy Thursday. Lent is a time to prepare for Easter by following Jesus more closely. The seasonal color of violet is used as a sign of penance.

## Easter

The Easter Season is preceded by a three-day celebration of the Paschal mystery called the **Triduum**. It starts with the celebration of the Lord's Supper on Holy Thursday and ends with evening prayer on Easter Sunday.

The Easter Season continues for fifty days until Pentecost. It is a time to remember your Baptism and to give thanks for the Resurrection of Jesus that saved all people from the power of sin and everlasting death. White or gold colors are used during this season as a sign of great joy.

## Ordinary Time

Ordinary Time is a season in two parts. The first is between the Christmas Season and the First Sunday of Lent. The second is between the Easter Season and Advent. Ordinary Time is the time to remember the works of Jesus and listen to his teachings. The color green is used during this season as a sign of hope and growth.

© Harcourt Religion

❓ **What is your favorite liturgical season?**

**Activity** Connect Your Faith

**Remember His Love** On the chart of seasons on the opposite page, design symbols to illustrate the saving actions of Jesus that are celebrated in each Church season.

# Prayer of Praise

 Let Us Pray

*Gather and begin with the Sign of the Cross.*

*Sing together the refrain.*

Shout for joy, joy, joy! Shout for joy, joy, joy!
God is love, God is light, God is everlasting!

"Shout for Joy" © 1982, Jubilate Hymns, Ltd.

**Leader:** God, our good Father, you sent Jesus, your Son, to rescue us from the power of sin and everlasting death. This is our song.

**All:** *Sing refrain.*

**Leader:** Jesus, you came into this world of darkness as the light. Your words of love touched those who were sick and weak. You forgave sinners and freed them from shame. This is our song.

**All:** *Sing refrain.*

**Leader:** Jesus, you died on the cross, a sacrifice of love to set us free from our sins. This is our song.

**All:** *Sing refrain.*

**Leader:** Jesus, you were raised from the dead and ascended into heaven. You sent the Spirit to be with us always. We hope to share eternal life with you. This is our song.

**All:** *Sing refrain.*

**Leader:** Let us pray.

*Bow your heads as the leader prays.*

**All:** **Amen.**

**A** **Work with Words**    Match each description in Column 1 with the correct term in Column 2.

**Column 1**

_____ **1.** A time of fasting and penance

_____ **2.** Celebrates the birth of Jesus

_____ **3.** Focuses on the Resurrection of Jesus

_____ **4.** Prepares for the coming of Jesus

_____ **5.** The suffering, death, Resurrection, and Ascension of Jesus

**Column 2**

**a.** Advent

**b.** Christmas

**c.** Paschal mystery

**d.** Lent

**e.** Easter

**B** **Check Understanding**    Write responses on the lines below. What is the focus of Ordinary Time? What liturgical color is used?

_____

_____

## Activity  Live Your Faith

**What Season Is It?**    Recall the liturgical season the Church is currently celebrating.

• Decide what you can do to celebrate this season now.

• Make a plan for the coming week.

# Family Faith

## Catholics Believe

- The Church year celebrates the Paschal mystery.

- The seasons of the liturgical year include Advent, Christmas, Lent, Easter, and Ordinary Time.

### ✝ SCRIPTURE

Read *Psalm 148:1–14* to praise the beauty of God's many wonderful creations.

**www.harcourtreligion.com**
For weekly Scripture readings and seasonal resources

## Activity
# Live Your Faith

**Notice Signs of the Season**   Take a family walk or hike to look for signs of the season. Listen to the sounds, look for changes, and take in the beauty of God's creation. Discuss how these signs of the season in nature reflect the liturgical season as well. Pray a simple prayer of thanks as you list each sign of the season. Then celebrate with a snack or meal.

# People of Faith

Bede was born in Sunderland, England. After he became a monk, Bede studied the Scriptures. He wrote many lessons about the Bible and explained ways to reform the Church. Bede also became an expert in the history of the English Church. When he realized that he was dying, Bede worked hard and finished translating the Gospel of John into English. The feast day of Saint Bede is May 25.

▲ **Saint Bede**
673–735

##  Family Prayer

O God, help us grow closer to you by our worship at the Eucharist, our learning of our Catholic faith, and our devotion to prayer. Amen.

© Harcourt Religion

*In Unit 6 your child is learning about* SACRAMENTS.

**CCC** *See Catechism of the Catholic Church 1067–1068, 1168–1171 for further reading on chapter content.*

# Chapter 17 The Seven Sacraments

## Let Us Pray

**Leader:** Lord, we see your mightiness in the works
you have done.

"May the glory of the LORD endure forever;
may the LORD be glad in these works!"

*Psalm 104:31*

**All:** Lord, we see your mightiness in the works
you have done. Amen.

© Harcourt Religion

## Activity Let's Begin

**I Will Remember** Juana's favorite time of year is spring. Every spring Juana and her *abuela,* or grandmother, would garden together. This spring was different. Abuela died during the winter, and Juana missed her very much.

One day Juana walked past the flower bed and noticed buds on the green shoots. "Those are the flowers from the bulbs Abuela and I planted in the fall!" she thought. "When I see them, I will remember that she is living with God now."

• What things remind you of the special people in your life when they are not with you?

179

# God's Love Is Present

 **Focus** What is a sacrament?

The flowers in Juana's garden were signs to her that her *abuela* still lived with God and was loved by him. God the Father sent Jesus into the world as a sign of his love for all people. He pointed the way to God for all who followed him.

Jesus welcomed people like Peter and Zacchaeus, and they changed their lives for him. Jesus showed people God the Father's forgiveness. He healed some and called others to serve God's people. Through Jesus' words and actions, many people experienced God's saving love. Jesus made God and his love present.

Jesus said this to his Apostles at the Last Supper.

 **SCRIPTURE**

No one comes to the Father except through me. If you know me, then you will also know my Father. From now on you do know him and have seen him.

*John 14:6–7*

It was only after Jesus' Resurrection that his Apostles began to understand who Jesus really was. Gradually, they came to understand that he was not just a sign of God—he really was God!

❓ **How did Jesus show God's saving love to the world?**

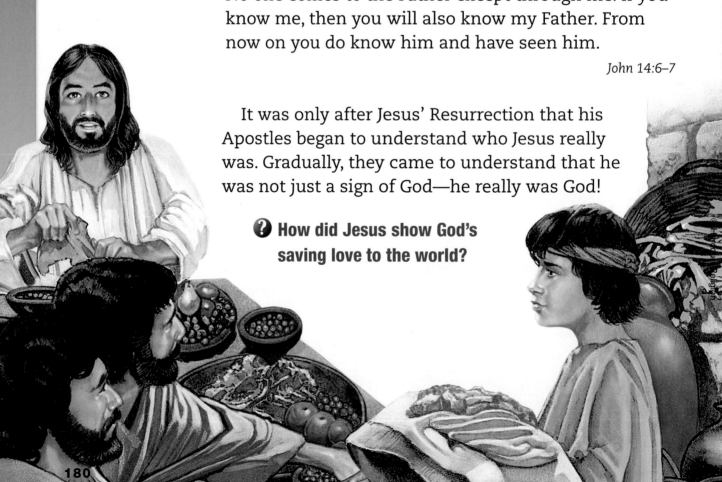

## Signs of God's Love

Jesus told his followers that he would always be with them and that they would continue his saving work. One of the ways that Jesus is with his people today is through the seven **sacraments**. The sacraments are actions of the Holy Spirit at work in Christ's Body, the Church. Jesus is present in the sacraments.

The Church has named seven sacraments that have their origins in Jesus. Each one celebrates a way that Jesus' saving work continues in the world.

### Words of Faith

The **sacraments** are signs that give grace. Sacraments were instituted by Christ and are celebrated by his Church.

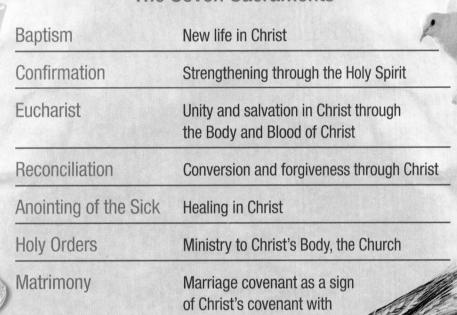

### The Seven Sacraments

| | |
|---|---|
| Baptism | New life in Christ |
| Confirmation | Strengthening through the Holy Spirit |
| Eucharist | Unity and salvation in Christ through the Body and Blood of Christ |
| Reconciliation | Conversion and forgiveness through Christ |
| Anointing of the Sick | Healing in Christ |
| Holy Orders | Ministry to Christ's Body, the Church |
| Matrimony | Marriage covenant as a sign of Christ's covenant with his Church |

## Activity — Share Your Faith

**Reflect:** Think of someone you love.

**Share:** Sketch a sign that reminds you of the person. Explain the sign to the class as you say the name.

**Act:** With your classmates, play a game matching the signs and names.

# Eucharist

 **Focus** What is the heart of the Christian life?

Jesus often ate meals with his friends. On the night before he died, Jesus shared a meal with his Apostles and asked them to remember him always.

## ✝ SCRIPTURE                                        Luke 22:17–20

# The Last Supper

Then [Jesus] took a cup, gave thanks, and said, "Take this and share it among yourselves; for I tell you [that] from this time on I shall not drink of the fruit of the vine until the kingdom of God comes." Then he took the bread, said the blessing, broke it, and gave it to them, saying, "This is my body, which will be given for you; do this in memory of me." And likewise the cup after they had eaten, saying, "This cup is the new covenant in my blood, which will be shed for you."

*Luke 22:17–20*

## Breaking of the Bread

After Jesus was raised from the dead and returned to the Father, his followers gathered weekly for a special meal. They called this meal the "breaking of the bread." They believed, as Catholics do today, that Jesus was present when they broke bread together. Today this meal is called the **Eucharist**, or Mass.

**❓ When did you first receive Jesus in Holy Communion? Tell what you remember about the day.**

# The Eucharist

The word *Eucharist* means "thanksgiving." At the beginning of Mass, you ask God's mercy because of your sins. Your venial sins can be forgiven through your celebration of the Eucharist. You listen to God's word. You thank God the Father for the great gift of his Son. When you receive Jesus in Holy Communion, you are united with the other members of the Body of Christ.

## Words of Faith

**Eucharist** is the sacrament through which Catholics are united with the life, death, and Resurrection of Jesus.

## Living the Eucharist

When Jesus told the Apostles to "do this in memory of me," he did not mean only that they should break bread together. He meant that they should live their lives as he did. Living the Eucharist means loving, welcoming, and forgiving others. You live the Eucharist when you share with those who do not have what you do.

❓ **What are some ways that you can live the Eucharist?**

## Activity  Connect Your Faith

**Dinner Guests**    Think of people you would like to have as company for dinner at your house, and write their names on the chairs. In the space on the table, write what you might do to welcome them and show them the love of Jesus.

# Prayer of Thanks

 Let Us Pray

*Gather and begin with the Sign of the Cross.*

| | |
|---|---|
| Reader: | The Lord be with you. |
| All: | **And also with you.** |
| Reader: | Lift up your hearts. |
| All: | **We lift them up to the Lord.** |
| Reader: | Let us give thanks to the Lord our God. |
| All: | **It is right to give him thanks and praise.** |
| Reader: | We are glad to give you thanks and praise because you love us. |

*Sing together.*

We come to share our story,
 we come to break the bread,
We come to know our rising from the dead.

"Song of the Body of Christ" © 2001, GIA Publications, Inc.

| | |
|---|---|
| Reader: | Because you love us, you gave us this great and beautiful world. |
| All: | *Sing refrain.* |
| Reader: | Because you love us, you sent Jesus your Son to bring us to you. |
| All: | *Sing refrain.* |
| Leader: | Let us pray. |
| | *Bow your heads as the leader prays.* |
| All: | **Amen.** |

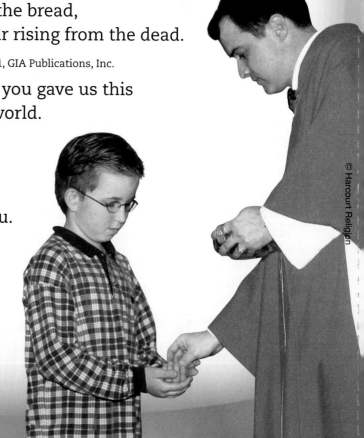

# Review and Apply

**A Check Understanding**   Circle True if a statement is true, and circle False if a statement is false. Correct any false statements.

1.   There are eight sacraments.

   True          False _____

2.   Jesus is present in all of the sacraments.

   True          False _____

3.   The early Christians did not celebrate the Eucharist.

   True          False _____

4.   Eucharist means "thanksgiving."

   True          False _____

5.   When you live the Eucharist, you continue Jesus' work in the world.

   True          False _____

**B Make Connections**   Why are the sacraments called saving actions?

_____

_____

_____

_____

_____

**Activity**   Live Your Faith

**Make a Eucharist Poster**   Create a poster for your parish bulletin board for people to see as they come to Mass.

• Title the poster "Living the Eucharist."

• On the poster, draw several ways people can live the Eucharist.

# Family Faith

## Catholics Believe

- The seven sacraments are signs, instituted by Christ, that give grace.
- The Sacrament of the Eucharist is at the heart of Christian life.

### ✝ SCRIPTURE

Read *Psalm 107* as a way to give thanks to God for his blessings.

**www.harcourtreligion.com**
For weekly Scripture readings and seasonal resources

## Activity

# Live Your Faith

**Create a Thank-you List**  In the Eucharistic Prayer you hear the words "Lift up your hearts" and "Let us give thanks to the Lord our God." Make a list of things for which you offer thanks to God. Remember these things the next time you participate in the Eucharist.

# People of Faith

 **Family Prayer**

**Margaret Mary Alacoque** was born into a peasant family in France. When she joined a convent, Margaret Mary developed a deep prayer life. She had several visions in which Jesus told her about his loving heart. Devotion to the Sacred Heart of Jesus, which includes participating in Mass and receiving the Eucharist on the first Friday of each month, developed and grew in the Church because of her inspiration. Her feast day is October 16.

▲ Saint Margaret Mary Alacoque 1647–1690

Saint Margaret Mary Alacoque, pray for us that we may deepen our prayer lives and our devotion to the Eucharist. Amen.

© Harcourt Religion

# Chapter 18 Healing and Reconciliation

## Let Us Pray

**Leader:** Merciful God, be always with us as we pray.

"Remember your compassion and love,
O Lᴏʀᴅ;
for they are ages old."

*Psalm 25:6*

**All:** Merciful God, be always with us as we pray. Amen.

## Activity Let's Begin

**Forgiveness** How would you complete these sentences?

• Forgiveness is easy when . . .

• Forgiveness is difficult when . . .

• I can always forgive . . .

• When I forgive, I . . .

• When I am forgiven, I . . .

# God's Forgiveness

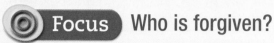

**Focus** Who is forgiven?

Jesus showed God's forgiveness to others through his words and actions. In this story, Jesus meets a wealthy tax collector who decides to become his follower.

## ✝ SCRIPTURE                                    Luke 19:1–10

# The Story of Zacchaeus

One day Jesus was passing through the town of Jericho. Zacchaeus, a rich tax collector, wanted to see Jesus and learn about him. Zacchaeus was short, so he climbed a tree to see past the crowd.

Jesus noticed Zacchaeus in the tree. He said, "Zacchaeus, come down quickly, for today I must stay at your house." Zacchaeus came down happily.

The crowd complained, saying that Jesus should not stay with Zacchaeus because Zacchaeus was a sinner.

Zacchaeus told Jesus that he would give money to those who were poor. He offered to give anyone he had cheated four times the amount of money that he owed to that person.

"Today salvation has come to this house," said Jesus. "For the Son of Man has come to seek and to save what was lost."

Based on *Luke 19:1–10*

❓ **Who has taught you the most about forgiveness? What did the person or persons say or do?**

© Harcourt Religion

# Turn to God

God is always ready and waiting to forgive. When you decide to turn away from sin and turn back toward God, you are experiencing conversion. God welcomes you back, just as Jesus welcomed Zacchaeus.

During his life Jesus forgave many people in his Father's name. After his Resurrection, Jesus told his disciples that he would send the Holy Spirit, who would give them the power to forgive sins. Today the Church continues to celebrate God's forgiveness in the **Sacrament of Reconciliation**. Sometimes this is called Penance or Confession. In this sacrament, you receive God's forgiveness of sins through the Church. The grace of this sacrament strengthens you to make peace with those whom you may have hurt.

© Harcourt Religion

## Words of Faith

The **Sacrament of Reconciliation** celebrates God's mercy and forgiveness and a sinner's reconciliation with God and with the Church through the absolution of the priest.

## Activity — Share Your Faith

**Reflect:** Think of someone who has forgiven you. Why did you need forgiveness?

**Share:** In groups discuss ways to show you are sorry and make peace with others.

**Act:** List two ways that you can be more forgiving of others.

_____

_____

189

# The Sacraments of Healing

 **Focus** How does the Church celebrate forgiveness and healing?

Celebrating the Sacrament of Reconciliation is a public sign that you are willing to turn away from sin and toward the love of God and the community. When you confess your sins to a priest, you ask for God's forgiveness through the power the Holy Spirit gives to the Church. God will forgive all sins, even mortal sins, if you are truly sorry and want to change your heart. When the priest says the words of **absolution**, you know that God has taken your sins away.

**❓ Why is it important to celebrate the Sacrament of Reconciliation?**

## Repairing the Harm

God forgives your sins, but the effects of your sins are still in the world. You must do what you can to repair the harm your sin has caused. Part of making up for your sin is to do the **penance** that the priest gives you.

## God's Healing Love

Today the Church anoints the sick or dying through the **Sacrament of the Anointing of the Sick** . This sacrament strengthens those who celebrate it and reminds them of God's healing love. God's love and forgiveness are available to all who turn to him.

In Jesus' time, people thought that sickness was God's punishment for someone's sin. But Jesus taught a different message.

### ✠ SCRIPTURE                          John 9:1–38

## The Man Born Blind

One day Jesus saw a man who had been blind from birth. His disciples asked him, "Why is this man blind? Is it because of his own sin or that of his parents?"

Jesus answered, "Neither he nor his parents sinned; it is so that the works of God might be made more visible through him."

Jesus rubbed clay on the man's eyes and told him to go to a certain place and wash it off. When the man did, he could see!

Many did not believe that Jesus had done this. When the man came back, Jesus asked the man, "Do you believe in the Son of Man? . . . You have seen him and the one speaking with you is he."

The man answered, "I do believe, Lord."

Based on *John 9:1–38*

## Words of Faith

Words of **absolution** are spoken by the priest during the Sacrament of Reconciliation.

**Penance** is the name for the prayer, offering, or good works the priest gives you in the Sacrament of Reconciliation.

The **Sacrament of the Anointing of the Sick** brings Jesus' healing touch to strengthen, comfort, and forgive the sins of those who are seriously ill or close to death.

### Activity   Connect Your Faith

**Think About Healing**   In the space below, name an illness that you've had or that someone you know has had. Then add the people and medicines or other things God has provided for healing.

_____

_____

# Prayer for Peace

 **Let Us Pray**

*Gather and begin with the Sign of the Cross.*

**Reader 1:** Merciful Father, we are together on earth, alone in the universe.

**All:** **Grant us peace, Lord.**

**Reader 2:** Look at us and help us love one another. Teach us to understand one another, just as you understand us.

**All:** **Grant us peace, Lord.**

**Reader 3:** Make our souls as fresh as the morning. Make our hearts as innocent as a baby's.

**All:** **Grant us peace, Lord.**

**Reader 4:** May we forgive one another and forget the past. And may we have peace within—and in our world today and forever.

**All:** **Grant us peace, Lord.**

**Leader:** Let us pray.

*Bow your heads as the leader prays.*

**All:** **Amen.**

*Sing together.*

Go now in peace.
Go now in peace.
May the love of God
surround you ev'rywhere,
ev'rywhere you may go.

"Go Now in Peace" ©1976 Hinshaw Music, Inc.

# Review and Apply

**Work with Words**   Use the clues to solve the puzzle.

**Down**

1. Welcoming someone back after a wrong has been done

2. These separate you from God and others.

3. This is done for those who are very sick or dying.

5. When you tell the priest your sins, you are really _____ to God.

**Across**

4. The sacrament that celebrates God's forgiveness of sins

6. When the priest says this, you know that God has taken your sins away.

7. Deciding to turn away from sin and turn back to God

8. This helps you make up for your sins.

9. _____ is always ready to forgive you.

10. Another name for Reconciliation

**Activity** **Live Your Faith**

**Share Forgiveness**   Think of a friend or family member who needs to hear a message of forgiveness from you. Create a card with a handwritten message, and deliver it to that person.

# Family Faith

## Live Your Faith

### Catholics Believe

- God's forgiveness is offered to all who seek it.

- The Sacraments of Reconciliation and the Anointing of the Sick celebrate God's healing love.

### ✝ SCRIPTURE

Read *Matthew 18:21–35* to learn from Jesus how we should forgive.

**Play the Yarn Game** Gather your family in a circle with a ball of yarn. Hold the end of the yarn in one hand and the ball in the other. Hold your end of the yarn and toss the ball to another person. Tell that person you are sorry for something that you did to him or her. Then that person repeats the action with someone else. Repeat the process until you weave a web of forgiveness with the yarn. Pray the Act of Contrition together.

**GO ONLINE** **www.harcourtreligion.com**
For weekly Scripture readings and seasonal resources

# People of Faith

▲ Venerable
Matt Talbot
1856–1925

**Matt Talbot** was born in Dublin, Ireland, to a family that was poor. As he grew up he developed a drinking problem. After years of heavy drinking, Matt decided to become sober. He had hurt and disappointed many of his friends and family members, but he asked their forgiveness. He prayed and practiced self-sacrifice. Matt gave most of his lumberyard wages to people who were poor or hungry. He made a better life for himself and many other people.

 **Family Prayer**

O God, give us the grace to overcome our shortcomings, and teach us to be self-sacrificing, as Matt Talbot was. Amen.

© Harcourt Religion

*In Unit 6 your child is learning about SACRAMENTS.*

**A** **Work with Words** Complete each sentence with the correct word. Then find the word in the word search.

```
k  c  b  l  y  e  c  n  a  n  e  p  o  q  r
i  z  y  w  g  n  n  s  t  m  n  w  r  c  a
t  e  s  a  c  r  a  m  e  n  t  s  d  n  e
e  e  k  n  d  i  m  h  o  t  l  r  i  n  y
f  u  z  o  r  e  s  j  l  o  g  t  n  k  l
o  c  b  a  n  o  i  n  t  i  n  g  a  i  a
p  h  u  n  c  z  o  l  e  i  e  w  r  c  c
k  a  q  i  z  i  f  i  j  r  m  h  y  d  i
y  r  e  t  s  y  m  l  a  h  c  s  a  p  g
b  i  z  n  n  x  y  k  s  v  s  r  d  g  r
m  s  z  g  f  a  d  t  w  b  r  k  a  n  u
z  t  n  i  x  m  u  u  d  i  r  t  h  p  t
k  k  z  f  o  r  g  i  v  e  n  e  s  s  i
x  a  w  e  o  x  s  i  b  j  k  e  f  g  l
k  n  o  i  t  a  i  l  i  c  n  o  c  e  r
```

1. The Sacrament of _____ strengthens you to make peace with those whom you may have hurt.

2. Absolution is spoken by a priest to communicate God's _____.

3. Jesus' healing touch strengthens and forgives the sins of those who are seriously ill in the Sacrament of the _____ of the Sick.

4. _____ is the sacrament through which Christians are united with the life, death, and Resurrection of Jesus.

5. The cycle of the Church's feasts and seasons is the

   _____.

6. Through the _____ Jesus saves us from sin and death.

7. _____ is a prayer or action the priest gives you to help you make up for the effects of your sins.

8. The _____ are signs that give grace.

9. The _____ celebrates the Passion, death, and Resurrection of Christ.

10. _____ Time is a season of the Church year.

**195**

# UNIT 7
## Judged on Love

### Chapter 19 A Generous Spirit

*What does it mean to have a generous spirit?*

### Chapter 20 The Church in the World

*What is the mission of the universal Church?*

### Chapter 21 I Want to See God

*When will you see God?*

 What do you think you will learn in this unit about being judged on love?

## Let Us Pray

**Leader:** Kindly God, your generous spirit amazes all your children.

"How good God is to the upright,
the Lord, to those who are clean of heart!"

*Psalm 73:1*

**All:** Kindly God, your generous spirit amazes all your children. Amen.

**Activity** Let's Begin

**The Giveaway**   Some Native Americans have a custom called *giveaway*. Instead of receiving gifts on his or her birthday, a person thinks of some personal possession that someone else has admired during the year. Then the person celebrating the birthday gives that possession to the person who has admired it. Native Americans say that this custom helps them show how grateful they are for the gifts of life and good fortune.

• What do you own that someone else has admired?

• How difficult would it be for you to give that possession away? Why?

© Harcourt Religion

Explore

# Desire for Riches

 **Focus** What does Jesus want you to know about riches?

Many cultures have stories that explore how much is too much. Here is one from ancient Greece.

A STORY

## KING MIDAS

Long ago and far away there lived in Greece a king named Midas. One day an old man wandered into King Midas's rose garden. Midas had his servants feed and care for the man.

Midas escorted the old man back to his home. The god Bacchus was pleased with the care Midas had given the man. Bacchus granted Midas one wish. Midas wished that everything he touched would turn to gold. And his wish was granted!

When he reached his palace, Midas ordered a feast to celebrate his good fortune. But when Midas tried to eat, his food turned to gold when he touched it. Midas soon grew hungry and thirsty, and he complained to his daughter. But when Midas's daughter hugged her father to console him, she also turned to gold!

❓ **What can you learn from the story of Midas?**

© Harcourt Religion

198

## Poor in Spirit

King Midas did not think of the consequences of his wish. Because Midas put his desire for riches first, he hurt himself and others.

Everything that God made is good. People are good. The things that people create with love and care are good. But Jesus taught that possessions are not the most important things. Do you remember the story found in *Matthew 19:16–22* about the rich young man? Jesus loved him and wanted him to be happy.

❓ **What did Jesus tell the rich young man to do?**

## First Things First

Sometimes people need to leave behind their material possessions in order to have the time and energy to do good. The Apostles left their homes, families, and jobs in order to follow Jesus and help him spread God's word.

The first beatitude says, "Blessed are the poor in spirit, for theirs is the kingdom of heaven" (*Matthew 5:3*). Those who do not become too attached to their possessions are able to work for love and peace in the world and help bring about God's kingdom.

### Faith Fact

In the Bible, the word *blessed* means "favored with the blessings of God."

**Activity** Share Your Faith

**Reflect:** Think about right and wrong choices for the following situations.

- A video game that you want is on an outdoor table during a sidewalk sale.
- Someone else wins an award that you wanted.

**Share:** In a small group, role-play one of these situations, showing how you could make a good choice.

**Act:** Write what you would do to make a good choice in the other situation. Why would this be a good choice?

© Harcourt Religion

# Living a Generous Life

 **Focus** What do the seventh and tenth commandments teach you?

There are two commandments that help you have the right attitude about material possessions. The seventh commandment says this: You shall not steal. The tenth commandment says this: You shall not covet your neighbor's goods.

Theft, greed, and envy are all sins against the seventh and tenth commandments. Theft is taking what is not yours. When you have **envy**, you resent or are sad because someone else possesses something that you really want. Envy harms the Body of Christ because it divides God's people rather than bringing everyone together. **Greed** is the desire to gain earthly possessions without concern for what is reasonable or right.

## An Open Heart

Humility, a spirit of generosity, and trust in God's care can help overcome envy and greed. If you are happy with what you have received, then you can be happy for the good fortune of others. Caring too much for things usually brings unhappiness and disappointment.

Because everything comes from God, all people have a right to what they need to live comfortably. As a member of the Body of Christ, you are called to share your possessions with others, especially those who do not have food, shelter, or decent clothing.

❓ **In what ways are people your age tempted to be envious or greedy?**

## Called to Stewardship

The seventh and tenth commandments require you to be generous with others. Being generous means giving more than is necessary.

God created the world for all creatures and called humans to stewardship. As stewards, or caretakers, people are called to use natural resources well and protect the environment for everyone now and in the future; to respect all life as a gift from God; and to share time, money, and talent to help others.

## Words of Faith

To **envy** is to resent or be sad from wanting for yourself what belongs to others.

**Greed** is the desire to acquire earthly goods without limit or beyond one's means.

### ✞ SCRIPTURE　　　　　　　Mark 12:41–44

## The Widow's Contribution

Jesus watched people put money into the temple treasury. Many rich people put in large sums of money. A poor widow put in two small coins worth only a few cents. Jesus said to his disciples, "I say to you, this poor widow put in more than all the others. They contributed their extra money, but the widow has given all she had."

Based on *Mark 12:41–44*

**❓ How did the widow contribute more than the rest?**

**❓ Who do you know who has a generous spirit?**

### Activity　Connect Your Faith

**Be a Good Steward**　Sketch a design for a stewardship ad that shows you or your group giving your time, talent, or treasure for the good of others. Encourage other people in your parish to share in similar ways.

# Prayer for Help

 Let Us Pray

*Gather and begin with the Sign of the Cross.*

Leader: God our Father, please hear our prayer. Help us see your Son in others.

All: **So that we may give freely and generously.**

Reader 1: Help us appreciate what we have been given.

All: **So that we may show gratitude to those who have been generous to us.**

Reader 2: Help us be happy when others have received gifts.

All: **So that we may be good friends to them.**

Reader 3: Help us remember others.

All: **So that we are willing to share our possessions.**

Leader: We ask for your guidance and continued love in Jesus' name by the grace of the Holy Spirit.

All: **Amen.**

*Sing together.*

For your gracious
blessing, for your
wondrous word, for
your loving kindness,
we give thanks, O God.

"For Your Gracious Blessing," Traditional.

**A** **Work with Words**   Complete the following statements.

1. The _____ states that you should not steal.

2. The responsibility to care for all of God's creation is _____.

3. The _____ states that you should not desire what others have.

4. When you _____ someone, you are resentful or sad that he or she possesses something that you want.

5. The unlimited gathering of material possessions is _____.

**B** **Check Understanding**   Explain how caring too much about possessions can get in the way of helping you cooperate with God's kingdom.

_____

_____

**Activity**   Live Your Faith

**Suggest Changes**   In each column, list several changes you would like to see happen for your family, friends, or community. Then make a resolution to help bring about one of these changes.

| Family | Friends | Community |
|--------|---------|-----------|
| _____ | _____ | _____ |
| _____ | _____ | _____ |
| _____ | _____ | _____ |

# Family Faith

## Catholics Believe

- The commandments call you to be generous and to have the right attitude toward possessions.

- The goods of the earth are meant for the benefit of the whole human family.

### SCRIPTURE

Read *2 Corinthians 9:6–9* to find out how the Corinthians were challenged to be generous.

**GO ONLINE** www.harcourtreligion.com
For weekly Scripture readings and seasonal resources

## Activity

# Live Your Faith

**Start a New Custom** Talk about the *giveaway* story at the beginning of this chapter.

- How hard would it be to add this custom to a birthday or to another celebration?

- In what other ways could you express a generous spirit toward others?

Choose one way, and decide how you will act on it as a family.

---

# People of Faith

▲ **Catherine de Hueck Doherty**
1900–1985

**Catherine de Hueck Doherty** was a Russian noblewoman who moved to Canada. She saw poverty in the world around her and decided to act. She founded the first Friendship House, a welcoming place for those who are poor. She then started Madonna House, a farm that combines prayer and a simple lifestyle. Since her death in 1985, Madonna Houses and Friendship Houses have continued to spread in the United States and Canada.

 **Family Prayer**

Jesus, help us imitate Catherine de Hueck Doherty's caring spirit as we learn how to share what we have with those in need. Amen.

*In Unit 7 your child is learning about the KINGDOM OF GOD.*

# Chapter 20 The Church in the World

## Let Us Pray

**Leader:** Giving God, thank you for the world you made and all the people who share it.

"How good it is, how pleasant,
   where the people dwell as one!"

*Psalm 133:1*

**All:** Giving God, thank you for the world you made and all the people who share it. Amen.

### Activity **Let's Begin**

**Different, Yet the Same**   Look around you. You are surrounded by differences. The people sitting in the room with you have different hairstyles, different eye colors, and different skin tones. They have different last names and may have different cultural backgrounds.

   And yet, with all these differences, you all belong to the same human family.

• With a partner, name all of the things that are the same for both of you. Then name all the ways that the two of you are different. Describe the most important thing that is the same for both of you and then the most important difference between you.

Harcourt Religion

# The Church in Bolivia

 **Focus** How does the Church include different cultures?

In the following story told by a Maryknoll missionary, you will find some ways that the Church in Bolivia is like your parish and some ways that it is different from your parish.

**A REAL-LIFE STORY**

## A Floating Church

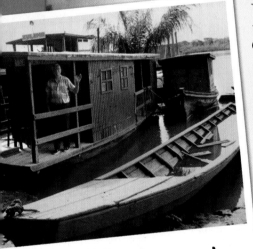

*Our Parish boat*

I work with other missionaries in the jungle region of northeast Bolivia. We travel in our parish boat to visit the people who live far apart along the Beni River. Most of the people work deep in the jungle. Some work with rubber trees, and others harvest Brazilian nuts. On our way up the river, we tell whoever is home to gather their neighbors together for Mass, Baptisms, and marriages on the day we will return downstream. When we return, the people gather near the river. There we baptize people, celebrate Mass, and perform marriages.

### The People

The people are happy to have us come and celebrate the sacraments with them. Ninety-five percent of Bolivians are Catholic. Their ancestors were converted to Christianity a long time ago. Many of the people we meet along the river still speak their native Indian languages. The people we meet also bring some of their native customs into their religious life.

❓ **What about the missionaries' experience in Bolivia is different from the experience in your parish?**

## The Mission

My coworkers and I have learned the languages of the people. We spend time talking and listening to the people. We are able to help them take care of their health in a clinic, and we educate them in a school. We have helped them set up a type of company called a *cooperative,* which is owned by the people who use its services. For example, we helped the farmers set up a cooperative so that they could get fair prices for their rubber and nut crops.

Bolivia has a lot of troubles. Once there was an uprising in a town, and one of the government people asked me to be mayor for four months. Another time I was arrested with another priest. We were put in jail because we had helped the people form a cooperative.

Our outdoor clinic

The Beni River

## Activity Share Your Faith

**Reflect:** Think about how the "floating church" is the same as your parish church.

**Share:** With a partner, use examples from the story to describe how the Church includes different cultures.

**Act:** Write one thing that you can do to support people in the Church who come from different cultures.

_____

_____

# To the Whole World

 **Focus** How does the Church reach out to the world?

Catholic missionaries bring the Catholic faith to people all over the world. They are careful to respect and include the customs of different groups in prayer and worship.

## Faith Fact

There are over 92,000 Catholic missionaries working around the world.

The missionaries in Bolivia are preaching the gospel of Jesus in word and deed. Before Jesus ascended into heaven, he gave his Apostles this command.

## SCRIPTURE
Matthew 28:18–20

## Go Forth

"All power in heaven and on earth has been given to me. Go, therefore, and make disciples of all nations, baptizing them in the name of the Father, and of the Son, and of the holy Spirit, teaching them to observe all that I have commanded you. And behold, I am with you always, until the end of the age."

*Matthew 28:18–20*

Jesus wanted his followers to go out to all places. Today, no matter where you go in the world, you will find followers of Jesus. In every country, you will find communities of Catholics and other Christians. Every one of these communities and all of the followers of Jesus are called to continue the **mission** of Jesus.

**?** How do you live out the mission of Jesus?

## Jesus' Universal Mission

Jesus' universal, or worldwide, mission on earth was to share God's love with all people. When you read the Scriptures, you see that Jesus reached out to all people, especially people who were poor and those who were left out by others. Jesus healed, forgave, and loved people, especially those people who were considered sinners. Jesus treated everyone with dignity and respect. Jesus' mission was one of **justice** .

## Diversity in the Church

There are differences in the way the people of other countries and cultures practice their faith. Even in your parish you may notice a **diversity** , or variety, in the ways that people express their faith. These differences do not divide the Church. They make it better. The Church is united because of its faithfulness to the common belief handed down from the Apostles through their successors, the bishops. The Church is united in the celebration of the Mass, in the sacraments, in prayer, and when people in every culture help bring justice to the world. You bring justice to the world by working to give others what is rightfully theirs.

❓ **What cultural practices does your parish or family have?**

### Words of Faith

To be sent on a **mission** means to be sent to share the good news of Jesus and the kingdom of God.

**Justice** is the virtue of giving to God and people what is due them.

**Diversity** means variety, especially among people.

## Activity Connect Your Faith

**Tell the World**   Write a newspaper headline that tells one way that you can bring justice to the world now or in the future.

_____

_____

# Prayer of Praise

 **Let Us Pray**

*Gather and begin with the Sign of the Cross.*

*Sing together.*

Go out to all the world, and tell the Good News.

"Psalm 117: Go Out to All the World" © 1969, 1981, and 1997, ICEL.

**Leader:** Lord, all the nations praise you. All the people of the world glorify you.

**All:** God our loving Father, we thank you for the gift of your Son, Jesus. We thank you for the beautiful diversity of our world. All nations and people show us your greatness. Fill us with your Spirit so that we can bring the good news of Jesus to all whom we meet. Amen.

**A** **Work with Words**    Complete each sentence by unscrambling the word in parentheses.

1. Jesus' (sonsimi) _____ was to share God's love with all people.

2. The Church is one, made up of a great (vidityers) _____ of members.

3. The mission of every person in the Church is to bring the good news of Jesus to the (lorwd) _____.

4. The virtue of (tcjuise) _____ challenges followers of Jesus to work to provide for the needs and rights of others.

5. Missionaries must (serpcet) _____ the culture and customs of the local people.

**B** **Check Understanding**    Write a response on the lines below. How can you bring justice to the world?

_____

_____

_____

## Activity  Live Your Faith

**Share Good News**    Take the good news statement that you created for the prayer service, print it on a card, and decorate it. How can you share this good news with someone this week? Write your idea, and act on it in the coming week.

To Do
- ☐ _____
- ☐ _____
- ☐ _____
- ☐ _____
- ☐ _____

# Family Faith

## Catholics Believe

- The mission of the People of God is to proclaim the Gospel and to work for the good of all people.

- The Church is made up of people of many cultures, but all are united by their belief in Christ.

### ✝ SCRIPTURE

Read *Ephesians 4:7–16* to find out about unity in diversity.

**GO ONLINE** www.harcourtreligion.com
For weekly Scripture readings and seasonal resources

## Activity

# Live Your Faith

**Research Religious Traditions** Share your experiences of different religious traditions. If possible, go online with a family member to research the religious traditions from a culture other than your own. Plan a special family time to tell what you discovered.

# People of Faith

▲ Cesar Chavez
1927–1993

As a child, **Cesar Chavez** was a migrant farm worker. As an adult, he improved working conditions for migrant workers and started the United Farm Workers union. Cesar had a deep Christian faith. He also followed the nonviolent teachings of Mohandas Gandhi and of Martin Luther King, Jr. He and other protesters often went to Mass together before they began a march. He organized strikes and boycotts to get fair wages for farm workers.

 Family Prayer

Dear God, give us a sense of justice and the courage to carry out your mission of justice in our world as Cesar Chavez did. Amen.

*In Unit 7 your child is learning about the KINGDOM OF GOD.*

### Chapter 21

# I Want to See God

## Let Us Pray

**Leader:** God, teach us to live so that we may share eternal life with you.

"Turn from evil and do good; seek peace and pursue it."

*Psalm 34:15*

**All:** God, teach us to live so that we may share eternal life with you. Amen.

## Activity

### Let's Begin

**With Jesus** Jessie sat with her mother in the car. Her mother wiped away Jessie's tears and said, "I will miss your Grandma Ruth, too. But she is happy and in heaven with Jesus."

When they arrived at the funeral home, Jessie gazed around the room where the body of her grandmother lay. Sweet-smelling flowers filled the room, and soft music played. With a huge gasp, Jessie declared, "Oh, so this is heaven!"

• What do you think heaven is like?

# Being with God

 **Focus** How do the gifts of the Holy Spirit help you live in friendship with God?

Heaven is not a room with sweet-smelling flowers. It is not a place in the sky among the clouds. **Heaven** is the life that all holy people will share with God forever.

To spend eternity with God, you first must grow in friendship with God. Through the Holy Spirit, God has given you gifts that will help you grow in friendship with him and with others. You receive the gifts of the Holy Spirit at Baptism, and in Confirmation these gifts are strengthened in you. These seven powerful gifts help you follow Jesus more closely. They open your heart so that the Holy Spirit can guide you to make good and unselfish choices.

| THE GIFT OF | HELPS YOU |
|---|---|
| WISDOM | • see yourself as God sees you and act as God wants you to act<br>• live in the image and likeness of God |
| UNDERSTANDING | • get to know God, yourself, and other people better<br>• see why you sometimes make wrong choices<br>• learn to make better choices<br>• learn to forgive more freely |
| COUNSEL (or right judgment) | • give good advice to others<br>• hear the Holy Spirit, who speaks to you through your conscience and through the good advice and good example of others |

| THE GIFT OF | HELPS YOU |
|---|---|
| **FORTITUDE** (or courage) | • stand up for what is right even when doing so is difficult<br>• face and overcome your fear, which is sometimes the reason why you make a bad choice or fail to act in loving ways |
| **KNOWLEDGE** | • be open to God's loving communication, or revelation<br>• know God in the way that you come to know someone you love and someone who loves you |
| **PIETY** (or reverence) | • show faithful love and honor to God<br>• recognize the importance of spending time talking and listening to God in prayer<br>• show respect to others because all people are children of God |
| **FEAR OF THE LORD** (or wonder and awe) | • know that God is greater and more wonderful than any created thing<br>• remember to be open to the surprising and powerful goodness of God |

## Words of Faith

**Heaven** is the state of eternal happiness with God.

## Activity — Share Your Faith

**Reflect:** Think about times when you used the gifts of the Holy Spirit.

**Share:** With a partner, discuss one of those times.

**Act:** Write one of these gifts in the box on the left, and describe how you use this gift in your everyday life.

# The Last Judgment

 **Focus** How does a person prepare for the last judgment?

The gifts of the Holy Spirit help you turn away from selfish actions and prepare you to be with God forever. All through your life you have the choice of accepting or rejecting the grace offered through Jesus. At the time of your death, God will judge how well you have accepted his gifts. This is called the **particular judgment**.

Jesus asks you to love God above all things and your neighbor as yourself. If you remain in God's grace and friendship by following his law, the everlasting happiness of heaven will eventually be yours. Some people sin greatly and reject God's covenant of love. They refuse his grace and forgiveness. These sinners will be separated forever from God because of their own choices. That separation is called *hell*.

At the end of time, all people who have ever lived will rise again and appear before God for judgment. This **last judgment** will not change each person's particular judgment. Rather, it will mark the coming of God's kingdom in its fullness. This is the time when Christ will come again in glory.

## Preparing for Heaven

When you live with the particular and last judgments in mind, you will try to work every day for the justice, love, and peace of God's reign. As you do so, you are preparing to live forever with God. Jesus told his followers what would happen on the day of the last judgment.

# The Last Judgment

"Then the king will say to those on his right, '. . . . Inherit the kingdom prepared for you. . . . For I was hungry and you gave me food, I was thirsty and you gave me drink, a stranger and you welcomed me, naked and you clothed me, ill and you cared for me, in prison and you visited me.' Then the righteous will answer him and say, 'Lord, when did we see you hungry and feed you, or thirsty and give you drink? When did we see you a stranger and welcome you, or naked and clothe you? When did we see you ill or in prison, and visit you?' And the king will say to them in reply, 'Amen, I say to you, whatever you did for one of these least brothers of mine, you did for me.' "

*Matthew 25:34–40*

## Words of Faith

**Particular judgment** is the individual judgment by God at the time of your death.

The **last judgment** will occur at the end of time when Jesus returns to judge all who have ever lived. Then, all will fully see and understand God's plan for creation.

❓ **Who is the king in this story?**

❓ **Who are the righteous in this story?**

**Activity** Connect Your Faith

**Express Yourself** Make a slogan for a bumper sticker about living according to how you will be judged. Then decorate the bumper sticker with markers or colored pencils.

# Prayer for the Kingdom

 **Let Us Pray**

*Gather and begin with the Sign of the Cross.*

**Leader:** Lord Jesus, you sometimes described heaven as a feast or a banquet. Help us remember the gift of your life and teaching that we have shared together this year. Be with us as we remember and pray.

*Share a story of Jesus that you remember from this year. Then pray together.*

**All:** **Lord Jesus, we long to see your face. May your kingdom come into our hearts and into our world. Open our hearts to those who are poor, sick, imprisoned, lonely, and suffering. Make us one Body in Christ through the gifts of your Spirit. Help us ready ourselves for the banquet of heaven. Amen.**

*Sing together.*

We come to share our story,
*Venimos a decir del misterio,*
we come to break the bread.
*y partir el pan de vida.*
We come to know our rising from the dead.
*Venimos a saber de nuestra eternidad.*

"We Come to Share Our Story" © 1989, GIA Publications, Inc.

**A** **Work with Words**   Complete each statement with the correct gift of the Holy Spirit.

1. Josh gives his best friend good advice, telling him not to shoplift. _____

2. Kim didn't do her homework, but she decides to tell her teacher the truth. _____

3. Tasha was ready to steal a CD. When she remembered what was talked about in religion class, she put the CD back. _____

4. Madison is overwhelmed with the beauty of the night sky and she thinks of God. _____

5. Amelia is struggling with a decision. She thinks about what Jesus would do. _____

**B** **Check Understanding**   In your own words, explain what will happen at the last judgment.

_____

_____

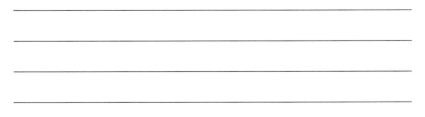

**Activity**  Live Your Faith

**Describe Your Life**   How do you want to be remembered by others after you leave your life on earth? In the space below, write a sentence that describes your life.

_____

_____

_____

_____

# Family Faith

## ◎ Catholics Believe

■ The Church teaches that at the end of time, all will be raised from the dead.

■ After being raised from the dead, all will come into the presence of Christ to be judged.

### ✝ SCRIPTURE

Read *Mark 7:31–37* to learn a story about Jesus' powerful ability to heal those who are suffering.

**GO ONLINE** www.harcourtreligion.com
For weekly Scripture readings and seasonal resources

## Activity
## Live Your Faith

**Think of Ways to Help** As a family, brainstorm ways in which people in the world are suffering. Look for newspaper articles and stories on the news. When you gather for dinner, pray for a person or about a situation in which there is suffering. Discuss how your family could help. If there is no direct action you can take, keep that person or situation in your family's prayers each day this week.

Daily News

## People of Faith

▲ Korean Saints and Martyrs 1839–1867

On May 6, 1984, the Church canonized 103 Korean people. These saints ranged in age from thirteen-year-old **Peter Yu Tae-chol** to seventy-two-year-old **Mark Chong**. Each of these people sacrificed his or her life for the sake of Jesus and the Catholic faith. Eleven of the martyrs were priests. Many of these saints were the first Christians in Korea, among them **Yi Sung-hun**, founder of the first Church community in that country. The feast day for these saints and martyrs is September 20.

## 🙌 Family Prayer

Saints and martyrs of Korea, pray for us that we will be strong in our faith even when it is difficult to do so. Pray that we may live wisely and lovingly to prepare to meet God at the end of time. Amen.

© Harcourt Religion

*In Unit 7 your child is learning about the KINGDOM OF GOD.*

# UNIT 7 REVIEW

**Work with Words**  Complete each sentence with the correct term.

1. To _____ or want for yourself what belongs to others is called envy.

2. Variety, especially among people, is known as

    _____.

3. The _____ will occur at the end of time, when Jesus returns to judge all who have ever lived.

4. The virtue of giving to God and people what is due them is called

    _____.

5. _____ is the desire to acquire earthly goods without limit or beyond one's means.

6. The _____ are those who do not become too attached to their possessions and are able to help bring about God's reign.

7. To share the good news of Jesus and the kingdom of God, people

    are sent on a _____.

8. _____ is the responsibility to care for all of God's creation.

9. The state of eternal happiness with God is known as

    _____.

10. _____ is the individual judgment by God at the time of a person's death.

# CATHOLIC SOURCE BOOK

## The Books of the Bible

The Catholic version of the Bible contains seventy-three books—forty-six in the Old Testament and twenty-seven in the New Testament.

### The Old Testament

#### The Pentateuch

| | | |
|---|---|---|
| Genesis | Leviticus | Deuteronomy |
| Exodus | Numbers | |

#### The Historical Books

| | | |
|---|---|---|
| Joshua | 2 Kings | Judith |
| Judges | 1 Chronicles | Esther |
| Ruth | 2 Chronicles | 1 Maccabees |
| 1 Samuel | Ezra | 2 Maccabees |
| 2 Samuel | Nehemiah | |
| 1 Kings | Tobit | |

#### The Wisdom Books

| | | |
|---|---|---|
| Job | Ecclesiastes | Sirach |
| Psalms | Song of Songs | (Ecclesiasticus) |
| Proverbs | Wisdom | |

## Faith Fact

Before the invention of the printing press, the Bible had to be copied by hand. Many times when copying the text, monks would also illuminate, or illustrate, Scripture passages.

© Harcourt Religion

## The Prophetic Books

| | | |
|---|---|---|
| Isaiah | Hosea | Nahum |
| Jeremiah | Joel | Habakkuk |
| Lamentations | Amos | Zephaniah |
| Baruch | Obadiah | Haggai |
| Ezekiel | Jonah | Zechariah |
| Daniel | Micah | Malachi |

# The New Testament

## The Gospels

## The New Testament Letters

| | | | |
|---|---|---|---|
| Matthew | Romans | 1 Thessalonians | James |
| Mark | 1 Corinthians | 2 Thessalonians | 1 Peter |
| Luke | 2 Corinthians | 1 Timothy | 2 Peter |
| John | Galatians | 2 Timothy | 1 John |
| | Ephesians | Titus | 2 John |
| | Philippians | Philemon | 3 John |
| | Colossians | Hebrews | Jude |

## The Acts of
## the Apostles

## Revelation

## Faith Fact

Each of the Gospel writers has a symbol. Matthew is represented by a winged man, Mark is represented by a winged lion, Luke is represented by a winged ox, and John is represented by an eagle.

## About the Old Testament

**The Pentateuch** is the first five books of the Old Testament. The word pentateuch means "five containers." In the beginning the pentateuch was written on leather or papyrus and each book was kept in a separate container. Jewish people call these books the Torah. The books of the pentateuch tell of the beginning of human relationship with God. They also tell the story of God's loving actions for humans.

The Wisdom books of the Old Testament provide guidance in human behavior. Wisdom is a spiritual gift that allows a person to know God's purpose and plan. They remind us that God's wisdom is always greater than human knowledge.

Many prophets were authors of Old Testament books. A prophet is a person sent by God to call people back to their covenant with God.

## The Formation of the New Testament

The New Testament was formed in three stages:

1. The life and teaching of Jesus—Jesus' whole life and teaching proclaimed the good news.
2. The oral tradition—After the Resurrection the Apostles preached the good news. Then the early Christians passed on what the Apostles had preached. They told and retold the teachings of Jesus and the story of his life, death, and Resurrection.
3. The four Gospels and other writings—The stories, teachings, and sayings of Jesus were collected and written down in the Gospels according to Matthew, Mark, Luke, and John. The actions and lessons of the early Church were recorded in the Acts of the Apostles and the New Testament letters.

## How to Locate Bible Passages

To practice finding a particular Bible passage, use the example of *Matthew 8:23–27.*

Matthew is the name of a book in the Bible. The chapter number always comes directly after the name of the book, so 8 is the chapter number. The numbers 23–27 refer to the verses. To find this passage, go to the table of contents in your Bible. Find the page number for the Gospel of Matthew, and turn to that page. The chapter number will be at the top of the page. Turn the pages to find Chapter 8. When you reach Chapter 8, look for the smaller numbers within the passage. These are the verse numbers. Find verse 23. This is where you will begin reading. Continue reading through verse 27, the last verse in the passage.

*Matthew* is the name of the book in the Bible.

The numbers *23–27* refer to the verses.

## The Covenant

**The covenant** is the sacred agreement joining God and humans in relationship. When God made the covenant with Noah after the flood, he promised never to destroy the earth again. God renewed the covenant with Abram (Abraham), promising that Abraham's descendants would be as numerous as the stars. Years later, when the descendants of Abraham were slaves in Egypt, God used Moses to lead the people away in the *Exodus,* or "the road out." At Mount Sinai the covenant was renewed with Moses. God guided the Israelites to the Promised Land. In return, the Israelites were called to love only God and to follow his Law, the Ten Commandments. Finally, through the Paschal mystery—Jesus' life, death, and Resurrection—the covenant was fulfilled and a new covenant was created. The new covenant is open to all who remain faithful to God.

# The Holy Trinity

God is revealed in three Persons: God the Father and Creator, God the Son and Savior, God the Holy Spirit and Guide. Each of the Persons of the Trinity is separate from the other Persons. However, the Father, Son, and Holy Spirit are one and the same God. The Holy Trinity is the central mystery of the Catholic faith.

The mission of God the Son and God the Holy Spirit is to bring people into the love of the Trinity—the perfect love that exists in the Father, Son, and Holy Spirit.

## God the Father

God created all things. The beauty of creation reflects the beauty of the Creator. He cares for and loves all. In his divine providence, God guides everything toward himself.

## God the Son

Jesus is the Son of God. The Church has many important teachings about him. The **Incarnation** is a basic mystery of the Catholic faith and is the belief that God became man. Jesus Christ became man in order to save all people from the power of sin and everlasting death. Jesus was truly man and yet was truly God. Jesus became human, being born of the Virgin Mary. Except for sin, Jesus had all the experiences of being human.

Through the teachings of Jesus, people come to know about the kingdom of God and how to live for God's reign. From the Sermon on the Mount and other teachings, people learn to live in love. Jesus did not reject sinners, but instead called them to turn away from sin and back to God. Jesus taught everyone how to live the Ten Commandments—by loving God and all of his creation.

## Faith Fact

The Holy Trinity is represented by many symbols, including the equilateral triangle, three interwoven circles, a circle of three fish, and the shamrock.

Jesus' **Resurrection** showed him as the Messiah, the Savior. By his death Jesus conquered sin. By rising from the dead, Jesus conquered death and so saved all humans from the power of sin and everlasting death.

The Ascension happened forty days after the Resurrection, when Jesus ascended to heaven to join the glory of God the Father. At the Ascension Jesus commanded the Apostles to continue his mission by teaching and guiding people toward God's kingdom. The sending of the Holy Spirit on Pentecost is the final part of Jesus' act of salvation.

## God the Holy Spirit

The Holy Spirit continues to guide people in the Christian life. Through the teachings of Jesus, Christians learned how to live in love. Through the strength and wisdom of the Holy Spirit, they are able to lead this life of love. The Holy Spirit breathes into the faithful his fruits and his gifts. The fruits—such as piety, peace, and joy—and the gifts—such as wisdom, courage, and reverence—help humans turn toward God and cooperate in bringing about the kingdom of God.

The **Immaculate Conception** means that Mary was preserved from original sin from the first moment of conception. The Feast of the Immaculate Conception is December 8. On this date, the Catholics of Paraguay celebrate the feast day of the Virgin of Caacupe. Centuries ago, the Virgin Mary appeared in the Paraguayan countryside. A church was built in the place where she had appeared, and many pilgrims to that church have experienced miracles. Today December 8 is as special a celebration to the Catholics of Paraguay as Christmas is. Many Paraguayans honor Mary every year by making a pilgrimage, or long walk, to the church of the Virgin of Caacupe.

© Harcourt Religion

## Faith Fact

The many titles for the Pope include: Bishop of Rome, Vicar of Christ, Supreme Pontiff of the Universal Church, Patriarch of the West, Primate of Italy, Successor of St. Peter, Prince of the Apostles, Servant of the Servants of God, and Sovereign of Vatican City.

# Church

Church **authority** is based on the command from Jesus to his Apostles to make disciples of people everywhere, teaching them to live as Jesus taught and baptizing them in the name of the Father, Son, and Holy Spirit. (See *Matthew 28:18–20*.) Authority also comes from the Holy Spirit as the Spirit of Truth that guides the Church. The official teaching authority of the Church is the **magisterium,** which is made up of the pope and the bishops. The magisterium teaches with the authority given by Jesus and the guidance of the Holy Spirit.

## Mission

The Church has the mission to help bring justice to everyone. The principles of social justice are respect for all persons, equality for all persons, and oneness in the family of God with responsibility for one another. These principles can be accomplished with the fair distribution of goods, fair wages for work, and fair resolution in conflicts.

## Pope

The pope's title of "Servant of the Servants" began with Pope Gregory the Great. It is stated in Mark 10:44 *"[W]hoever wishes to be first among you will be the slave of all."*

## Saints

Canonization is the process by which the Church recognizes faithful people as saints. During each of the three stages of becoming a saint, the faithful person has a different title—first Venerable, then Blessed, and finally Saint.

# Last Things

## Purgatory

At death some people are not ready for heaven and God's eternal friendship. However, they have not broken their relationship with God. These souls are given time in purgatory. *Purgatory* means "purifying." Purgatory helps the soul prepare for life with God. The soul becomes more faithful and loving.

## Particular judgment

When people die, they are judged by how well they have lived and loved. This judgment is called particular judgment. Souls will be given reward or punishment at this time.

## General judgment

General judgment, or the last judgment, will occur at the Second Coming of Christ. This judgment represents God's triumph over evil. General judgment will mark the arrival of God's kingdom in its fullness. General judgment will happen to all people, living and dead. However, this judgment will not change the particular judgment received by each soul.

# Liturgy

# The Liturgical Year

**Advent**
Four Sundays of Advent

**Christmas Season**
Christmas Day
Feast of the Holy Family
Feast of Epiphany

**Ordinary Time I**
Sundays between Epiphany and Ash Wednesday

**Ordinary Time II**
Sundays between Pentecost and the First Sunday of Advent

**Lent**
Ash Wednesday, Five Sundays of Lent, and Passion, or Palm, Sunday

**Triduum**
Holy Thursday, Good Friday, Holy Saturday, Easter Sunday

**Pentecost**
Fifty days after Easter

**Easter Season**
Easter Sunday, Second through Seventh Sundays of Easter, and Pentecost Sunday

## Lent

Lent is a time of fasting, prayer, and almsgiving. The forty days of Lent remind Christians of the number of days Jesus spent fasting in the desert. The forty days also represent the number of years the Israelites spent wandering in the desert after the Exodus.

Lent begins with Ash Wednesday, a day of penance. The last Friday in Lent, Good Friday, is also a day of penance. All Catholics from their eighteenth to their fifty-ninth birthdays must fast on days of penance: They eat light meals and have no food between meals. On Ash Wednesday and on all Fridays during Lent, abstinence is required for Catholics fourteen years of age or older. This means that they may not eat meat. Fasting, abstinence, and personal reflection during Lent help prepare Catholics for the celebration of Easter.

## The Triduum

The *Triduum*, which means "three days," starts with the celebration of the Lord's Supper on Holy Thursday. Good Friday is observed with a Liturgy of the Word, Veneration of the Cross, and a Communion service. On Holy Saturday evening the Easter Vigil is celebrated. The Triduum ends with evening prayer on Easter Sunday. Because the Triduum celebrates the Paschal mystery—the life, death, and Resurrection of Jesus—it is the high point of the entire Church year.

### Faith Fact

The palms from Palm Sunday are collected and burned. The ashes are then used for the following year's Ash Wednesday service.

239

# The Sacraments

The Catholic Church celebrates seven sacraments, or signs, of Jesus' presence. There are three groups of sacraments.

| | |
|---|---|
| **Sacraments of Initiation** | Baptism Confirmation Eucharist |
| **Sacraments of Healing** | Reconciliation Anointing of the Sick |
| **Sacraments of Vocation and Service** | Matrimony Holy Orders |

## Holy Water

Holy water is water that has been blessed. It is used during the Sacrament of Baptism as well as for the blessing of people or objects. Fonts of holy water are placed at the entrances of churches so that people may bless themselves and recall the meaning of Baptism as they make the Sign of the Cross.

## The Paschal Candle

The Paschal candle is a symbol of Christ and of Easter. This candle is lit from the Easter fire during the Easter Vigil. Throughout the fifty days of the Easter Season, the candle burns during the liturgy. After the Easter Season it is used during baptisms and funerals as a symbol of the Resurrection.

# The Sacrament of Reconciliation

The Sacrament of Reconciliation is also known as the Sacrament of Penance or the Sacrament of Confession. In this sacrament, sin is forgiven and the one who has sinned is reconciled with God, with himself or herself, and with the Church community. The essential elements for Reconciliation are

- contrition (sorrow for the sin)
- confession
- absolution by the priest
- satisfaction (attempting to correct or undo the wrong done). The priest can never reveal what he is told during a confession. The priest's silence is called the *sacramental seal* or the *seal of confession*.

## Celebrating the Sacrament

## Communal Rite of Reconciliation

1. Greeting
2. Celebration of the Word
3. Homily
4. Examination of Conscience
5. General Confession of Sin
6. The Lord's Prayer
7. Individual Confession of Sins, Acceptance of a penance, and Absolution
8. Closing Prayer

## Individual Rite of Reconciliation

1. Welcome
2. Reading from Scripture
3. Confession of Sins and Acceptance of a Penance
4. Act of Contrition
5. Absolution
6. Closing Prayer

© Harcourt Religion

# Morality

## The Beatitudes

The Beatitudes are sayings of Jesus that show us the way to true happiness in God's kingdom. The Beatitudes are listed in the Gospel according to Matthew (*Matthew 5:3–10*), see Chapter 7.

## The New Commandment

Jesus also gave his followers a new commandment: "love one another. As I have loved you, so you also should love one another." (*John 13:34*).

# The Ten Commandments

### Faith Fact

The eight points on the Maltese Cross represent the Beatitudes.

| THE TEN COMMANDMENTS | THEIR MEANING |
|---|---|
| 1. I am the Lord your God. You shall not have strange Gods before me. | Keep God first in your life. |
| 2. You shall not take the name of the Lord your God in vain. | Always use God's name in a reverent way. |
| 3. Remember to keep holy the Lord's day. | Attend Mass and rest on Sunday. |
| 4. Honor your mother and father. | Obey your father and mother. |
| 5. You shall not kill. | Care for yourself and others. |
| 6. You shall not commit adultery. | Be respectful of every person. |
| 7. You shall not steal. | Respect other people and their property. |
| 8. You shall not bear false witness against your neighbor. | Respect others by always telling the truth. |
| 9. You shall not covet your neighbor's wife. | Don't be jealous of other people's relationships. |
| 10. You shall not covet your neighbor's goods. | Don't be jealous of what other people have. |

# Conscience

Conscience is the gift from God that helps you know the difference between right and wrong. Conscience helps you choose what is right. It involves free will and reason working together. You must form your conscience properly. If not formed properly, your conscience can lead you to choose what is wrong.

Forming your conscience is a lifelong process. It involves practicing virtues and avoiding sin and people or situations that may lead you to sin. You can turn to good people for advice, to Church teachings for guidance, and to God for help in educating your conscience.

## Examining Your Conscience

For help with examining your conscience, use the following steps:

1. Pray for the Holy Spirit's help in making a fresh start.

2. Look at your life in the light of the Beatitudes, the Ten Commandments, the Great Commandment, and the precepts of the Church.

3. Ask yourself these questions: Where have I fallen short of what God wants for me? Whom have I hurt? What have I done that I knew was wrong? What have I not done that I should have done? Have I made the necessary changes in bad habits? What areas am I still having trouble with? Am I sincerely sorry for all my sins?

# Law

Laws are rules that help people live as members of a community and behave in an acceptable manner.

**Divine law** is the eternal law of God. It includes physical law and moral law. The law of gravity is an example of physical. A moral law is one that humans understand through reasoning (you may not steal) and through divine revelation (keep holy the Lord's Day).

**Natural moral law** consists of those decisions and duties that all humans accept as right. For example, people everywhere understand that no one may kill another unjustly. Everyone must obey natural moral law.

## Precepts of the Church

The following precepts are important duties of all Catholics.

1. Take part in the Mass on Sundays and holy days. Keep these days holy and avoid unnecessary work.
2. Celebrate the Sacrament of Reconciliation at least once a year.
3. Receive Holy Communion at least once a year during Easter Season.
4. Fast and abstain on days of penance.
5. Give your time, gifts, and money to support the Church.

## Corporal Works of Mercy

These works of mercy help care for the physical needs of others.

Feed the hungry.
Give drink to the thirsty.
Clothe the naked.
Shelter the homeless.
Visit the sick.
Visit the imprisoned.
Bury the dead.

## Faith Fact

Pope John XXIII listed food, clothing, shelter, health care, rest, and social services as basic human needs. All people have a right to those basic needs.

WELCOME

236

© Harcourt Religion

## Human Dignity

God's image is his likeness that is present in you because you are his creation. You are called to respect the dignity of all people because everyone is made in God's image.

## Freedom

Freedom means you are able to choose and act with few limitations.

## Free will

Free will is the gift from God that allows humans to make their own choices. Because you are free to choose between right and wrong, you are responsible for your choices and actions.

## Grace

God gives you two types of grace. **Sanctifying grace** is the gift of God's life in you. It gives you the desire to live and act within God's plan. **Actual grace** is the gift of God's life in you that helps you think or act in a particular situation according to God's plan. Actual grace opens you to understanding and strengthens your will.

## Gifts of the Holy Spirit

You receive the gifts of the Holy Spirit through the Sacraments of Baptism and Confirmation. These gifts help you grow in relationship with God and others.

| | |
|---|---|
| Wisdom | Knowledge |
| Understanding | Reverence (*Piety*) |
| Right judgment (*Counsel*) | Wonder and awe (*Fear of* |
| Courage (*Fortitude*) | *the Lord*) |

# Sin

Sin is a turning away from God and a failure to love others. Sin affects both the individual and the community. A person may be sorry for his or her sin, ask forgiveness for it, accept punishment for it, and resolve to do better. In this case, the experience may actually help the person develop as a Christian and avoid sin in the future. However, a person who makes a habit of sin will harm his or her development, set a poor example, and bring sorrow to others. Society suffers when people disobey God's law and the just laws of society. There are many types of sin.

**Original sin** is the human condition of weakness and the tendency toward sin that resulted from the first humans' choice to disobey God. Baptism restores the relationship of loving grace in which all people were created.

**Actual sin** is any thought, word, act, or failure to act that goes against God's law. Sin is always a choice, never a mistake.

**Mortal sin** separates you from God. A mortal sin is an act, such as murder. There must be a deliberate choice to commit the act; it is never an accident.

**Venial sin** does not destroy your relationship with God, but it does weaken the relationship. Venial sin often comes from bad habits. It can lead to mortal sin.

**Social sin** happens when one person's sins affect the larger community. Poverty and racism are examples of social sin.

## Faith Fact

The word *virtue* means "strength." Practicing virtue can give you the strength to make loving choices.

# Virtue

Virtues are good qualities or habits of goodness. These are the two types of virtues:

| Theological Virtues | Cardinal Virtues |
| --- | --- |
| Faith | Prudence (careful judgment) |
| Hope | Fortitude (courage) |
| Love | Justice (giving people their due) |
| | Temperance (moderation, balance) |

# The Sign of the Cross

In the name of the Father, and of the Son, and of the Holy Spirit. Amen.

# The Lord's Prayer

Our Father,
who art in heaven,
hallowed be thy name;
thy kingdom come;
thy will be done on earth
as it is in heaven.
Give us this day our
daily bread;
and forgive us our
trespasses
as we forgive those who trespass
against us;
and lead us not into temptation,
but deliver us from evil. Amen.

# Hail Mary

Hail, Mary, full of grace,
the Lord is with you!
Blessed are you among women,
and blessed is the fruit of your womb, Jesus.
Holy Mary, Mother of God,
pray for us sinners,
now and at the hour of our death. Amen.

# Glory to the Father (Doxology)

Glory to the Father, and to the Son, and to the Holy Spirit:
as it was in the beginning, is now, and will be for ever. Amen.

# Apostles' Creed

I believe in God, the Father
   almighty,
creator of heaven and earth.
I believe in Jesus Christ, his
   only Son, our Lord.
He was conceived by the
   power of the Holy Spirit,
and born of the Virgin Mary.
He suffered under Pontius
   Pilate,
was crucified, died, and was
   buried.
He descended to the dead.
On the third day, he rose
   again.

He ascended into heaven,
and is seated at the right
   hand of the Father.
He will come again to judge
   the living and the dead.
I believe in the Holy Spirit,
the holy Catholic Church,
the communion of saints,
the forgiveness of sins,
the resurrection of the body,
and the life everlasting.
Amen.

## Faith Fact

*Amen* means "So be it."
Isn't that the perfect way
to end a conversation
with God?

# Nicene Creed

We believe in one God,
   the Father, the Almighty,
   maker of heaven and earth,
   of all that is seen and
   unseen.
We believe in one Lord, Jesus
   Christ,
   the only Son of God,
   eternally begotten of
      the Father,
   God from God, Light
      from Light,
   true God from true God,
   begotten, not made,
   one in Being with
      the Father.
   Through him all things
      were made.
   For us men and for
      our salvation
   he came down from
      heaven:
   by the power of the
      Holy Spirit
   he was born of the
      Virgin Mary,
   and became man.
For our sake he was crucified
   under Pontius Pilate;
   he suffered, died, and
      was buried.
   On the third day he
      rose again

in fulfillment of the
   Scriptures;
he ascended into heaven
and is seated at the
   right hand
of the Father.
He will come again in glory
   to judge the living and
      the dead,
   and his kingdom will
      have no end.
We believe in the Holy Spirit,
   the Lord, the giver of life,
   who proceeds from the
      Father and the Son.
   With the Father and
      the Son
   he is worshiped and
      glorified.
   He has spoken through
      the Prophets.
We believe in one holy
   catholic and apostolic
   Church.
We acknowledge one
   baptism
for the forgiveness of sins.
We look for the
   resurrection of the dead,
   and the life of the world
      to come.
Amen.

# I Confess/Confiteor

I confess to almighty God,
and to you, my brothers and sisters,
that I have sinned through my own fault
in my thoughts and in my words,
in what I have done,
and in what I have failed to do;
and I ask blessed Mary, ever virgin,
all the angels and saints,
and you, my brothers and sisters,
to pray for me to the Lord our God.

# Prayer to the Holy Spirit

Come, Holy Spirit, fill the hearts of your faithful.
And kindle in them the fire of your love.
Send forth your Spirit and they shall be created.
And you will renew the face of the earth.
Let us pray.
Lord, by the light of the Holy Spirit you have taught the
hearts of your faithful. In the same Spirit help us to relish
what is right and always rejoice in your consolation. We ask
this through Christ our Lord. Amen.

# Memorare

Remember, most loving Virgin Mary, never was it heard that
anyone who turned to you for help was left unaided. Inspired
by this confidence, though burdened by my sins, I run to your
protection for you are my mother. Mother of the Word of God,
do not despise my words of pleading but be merciful and
hear my prayer. Amen.

# WORDS OF FAITH

## A

**absolution** Words spoken by the priest during the Sacrament of Reconciliation. (191)

**authority** The power and the responsibility to lead others. (136)

## B

**Beatitudes** Teachings of Jesus that show the way to true happiness and tell the way to live in God's kingdom now and always. (97)

**blasphemy** The sin of showing contempt for the name of God, Jesus Christ, Mary, or the saints in words or action. (113)

## C

**canonized** Officially proclaimed a saint by the Church. Canonized saints have special feast days or memorials in the Church's calendar. (128)

**capital punishment** Taking the life of a person as punishment for a serious crime, such as murder. It is also called the death penalty. (156)

**charity** The virtue of love. It directs people to love God above all things and their neighbor as themselves, for the love of God. (105)

**community** A group of people who hold certain beliefs, hopes, and goals in common. (77)

**conscience** The gift from God that helps us know the difference between right and wrong and helps you choose what is right. (87)

**conversion** The process of turning our lives away from sin and toward the love of God and others. (189)

**Corporal Works of Mercy** Actions that meet the physical needs of others. (105)

**covenant** Sacred promise or agreement between God and humans. (53)

## D

**dignity** Is self worth. Every human is worthy of respect because he or she is made in the image of God. (69)

**diversity** means variety, especially among people. (209)

## E

**envy** To resent or be sad from wanting for yourself what belongs to others. (201)

**Eucharist** The sacrament through which Catholics are united with the life death and Resurrection of Jesus. (183)

## F

**faithful** To be steadfast and loyal in your commitment to God, just as he is faithful to you. (53)

**false witness** A misrepresentation of the truth. (164)

**forgiveness** An act of welcoming someone back after he or she has done wrong. Forgiveness includes accepting the person, even though you do not approve of the wrong behavior. *(189)*

**free will** The God-given ability to choose between good and evil. *(85)*

**gifts of the Holy Spirit** Seven powerful gifts we receive in Baptism and Confirmation. These gifts help us grow in our relationship with God and others. *(214–215)*

**grace** The gift of God's life in you. *(85)*

**Great Commandment** The two-fold command to love God above all and your neighbor as yourself. *(103)*

**greed** The desire to acquire earthly goods without limits or beyond one's needs. *(201)*

**heaven** The state of eternal happiness with God. *(215)*

**holiness** Being what God created you to be. You become holy, or Godlike, by sharing God's life of grace. *(128)*

**idolatry** The sin of worshiping an object or a person instead of God. It is letting anything or anyone become more important than God. *(111)*

**Immaculate Conception** The title for Mary that recognizes that God preserved her from sin from the first moment of her life. *(131)*

**justice** The virtue of giving to God and people what is due them. *(209)*

**kingdom of God** God's rule of peace, justice, and love that is here now, but has not yet come in its fullness. *(121)*

**laity** Name for all of the baptized people in the Church who share in Christ's mission but are not priests or consecrated sisters and brothers. *(123)*

**last judgment** The judgment that will occur at the end of time when Jesus returns to judge all who have ever lived. Then, all will fully see and understand God's plan for creation. *(217)*

**liturgical year** The cycle of feasts and seasons that makes up the Church's year of worship. *(173)*

**magisterium** The Church's teaching authority to interpret the word of God found in Scripture and Tradition. *(139)*

**martyr** A person who gives up his or her life to witness to the truth of the faith. *(163)*

**mission** To be sent to share the good news of Jesus and the Kingdom of God. (209)

**modesty** The virtue that helps people dress, talk, and act in appropriate ways. (149)

**morality** Living in right relationship with God, yourself and others. It is putting your beliefs into action. (79)

**mortal sin** A serious sin that destroys your relationship with God. (70)

**murder** The deliberate killing of an innocent person. (157)

**obey** To do things or act in certain ways that are requested by those in authority. (149)

**original sin** The choice of the first humans to disobey God. (51)

**parish** A Catholic community with shared spiritual beliefs and worship. (79)

**particular judgment** The individual judgment by God at the time of your death. (217)

**Paschal mystery** The mystery of Jesus' suffering, death, Resurrection, and Ascension. (173)

**patron saint** A model of faith and protector for you. (131)

**penance** The name for the prayer, offering, or good work the priest gives you in the Sacrament of Reconciliation. (191)

**perjury** A lie that is told in a court of law. (164)

**precepts of the Church** Some of the minimum requirements given by Church leaders for deepening your relationship with God and the Church. (139)

**providence** God's loving care for all things; God's will and plan for creation. (45)

**reparation** The action taken to repair the damage done through a sin. (165)

**revelation** The way God tells humans about himself and makes his plan known. (45)

**Sacrament of the Anointing of the Sick** Brings Jesus' healing touch to strengthen, comfort, and forgive the sins of those who are seriously ill or close to death. (191)

**Sacrament of Reconciliation** The sacrament that celebrates God's mercy and forgiveness and a sinner's reconciliation with God and the Church through the absolution of the priest. *(189)*

**sacraments** Signs that give grace. Sacraments were instituted by Christ and are celebrated by his Church. *(181)*

**saint** A person whom the Church declares has led a holy life and is enjoying eternal life with God in heaven. *(129)*

**Scripture** Another name for the Bible. Scripture is the word of God written in human words. *(45)*

**sin** The deliberate thought, word, deed, or omission contrary to the law of God. *(71)*

**social sin** A sinful social structure or institution that builds up over time so that it affects the whole society. *(71)*

**soul** The spiritual part of a human that lives forever. *(69)*

**stewardship** The human responsibility to care for God's creation and to respect all life as a gift from God. *(201)*

**suicide** The taking of one's own life. *(156)*

**Ten Commandments** The summary of laws that God gave to Moses on Mount Sinai. They tell us what is necessary in order to love God and others. *(60)*

**Triduum** The celebration of the Passion, death and Resurrection of Christ. The Triduum begins on Holy Thursday evening and concludes on Easter Sunday night. *(175)*

**venial sin** A less serious sin that weakens your relationship with God. *(70)*

**vocation** God's call to love and serve him and others. *(121)*

**vows** Solemn promises that are made to or before God. *(149)*

**worship** To adore and praise God especially in prayer and in liturgy. *(111)*

Note: Boldfaced numbers refer to pages on which the terms are defined.

Joan of Arc, Saint, 168
John, Saint, 224
John the Baptist, Saint, 15
John of God, Saint, 82
John XXIII, Pope, 129, 236
Jonah and the Big Fish, 44–45
Joseph, husband of Mary, 147
Joseph, son of Jacob, 58
Judah, 58
judgment, 39, 214, 216–217, 229
justice, **209**, 228, **243**

Kateri Tekakwitha, Blessed, 134
Katharine Drexel, Saint, 108
kingdom of God, 78, **121**, 216–217, 226, **243**
knowledge, 39, 215, 237

laity, 122–**123**, **243**
last judgment, 216–**217**, 229, **243**
Last Supper, 180, 182–183
    See also Eucharist
leadership, 20–23
Lent, 24–27, 174, 175, 230, 231
light, 32, 35
liturgical year, **173**–175, 230, **243**
Liturgy of the Word, 231
Lord's Day, 113
Lord's Prayer, 239
Lord's Supper, 231
love
    connection to God through, 68, 70–71
    of enemies, 157
    of family, 145–149
    as Great Commandment, 102–105
    of others, 76–79, 86–87, 120–123
    signs of, 180–181
    Ten Commandments and, 60–61
Luke, Saint, 224
lying, 164–165

Magi, 16, 19
magisterium, 138–**139**, 228, **243**
Margaret Mary Alacoque, Saint, 186
Mark, Saint, 224
Mark Chong, Saint, 220
marriage, 148, 181, 232
Martin de Porres, Saint, 100
martyrs, 90, 162–**163**, 168, 220, **243**
Mary, Mother of God, 8–11, 48, 130–131,
    147, 226, 227
Mary Magdalen Postel, Saint, 142
Mass, 182–183
material possessions, 102–103, 197–201
Matrimony, Sacrament of, 148, 181, 232
Matthew, Saint, 224
Maximilian Kolbe, Saint, 160
Memorare, 240
Miriam, 64
mission, 206–**209**, 228, **244**
missionaries, 206–209
modesty, **149**, **244**
morality, 78–79, 86–87, 234–238, **244**
mortal sin, **70**, 190, 238, **244**
Moses, 59–61, 64, 110–112, 155, 225
Mount Sinai, 60, 110, 225
murder, 70, 156–**157**, **244**

Naomi, 56
natural moral law, **236**
New Testament, 45, 223, 224
Noah, 51, 225
Nobel, Alfred, 154–155

obey, 53, 148–**149**, **244**
Old Testament, 45, 222–223, 224
Ordinary Time, 8, 20–23, 174, 175, 230
original sin, 50–**51**, 227, 238, **244**

Palm Sunday, 231
Paraguay, 227
parish, **79**, **244**
Parks, Rosa, 68–69, 71
particular judgment, 216–**217**, 229, **244**
Paschal mystery, **173**–175, 225, 231, **244**
patron saint, **131**, **244**
Paul, Saint, 20–23
peace, 227
penance, 139, 181, 189–**191**, 231, 233, **244**
Pentateuch, 222, **224**
Pentecost, 36–39, 138, 175, 230
perjury, **164**, **244**
Peter, Saint, 136–138, 180
Peter Yu Tae-chol, Saint, 220
piety (reverence), 39, 215, 227, 237
pope, 138, 228
prayer, 24, 85, 231, 239–241 See also prayers
    at the beginning and end of each lesson
precepts of the Church, **139**, 236, **244**
prophet, 224
Prophetic books, 223
providence, 44–**45**, **244**
pruning, **24**
psalms, 46, 62
purgatory, **229**

reconciliation, 139, 181, 188–191, 233
Reconciliation, Sacrament of, 139, 181,
    **189**–190, 232, 233, 245
reign of God, 121–123
reparation (satisfaction), 164–**165**, **244**
respect
    for God, 102–103, 110–113
    for life, 154–157
    for others, 70–72, 79, 112, 113, 237
revelation, **45**, **244**
reverence (piety), 39, 215, 227, 237
rich young man, 102
right judgment (counsel), 39, 214, 237
Ruth, 56

sacramental seal, 233
sacraments, 85, 173, **181**–183, 189–191,
    232–233, **245**
saint, 128–**129**, 229, **245**
    See also individual saint by name
salvation, 173, 188
sanctifying grace, **237**
Sarah, 53
Satan, 50
satisfaction (reparation), 164–165, 233
Saul, 20–23
Scripture, **45**, 87, 222–225, **245**
    See also Bible; New Testament; Old
    Testament
seal of confession, 233
Second Coming of Christ, 216–217, 229
Sermon on the Mount, 96–97, 226
Service, Sacraments of, 232
service/serving, 36–39, 121–123
Sign of the Cross, 112, 239
sin, 70–**71**, **245**
    forgiveness for, 28, 32, 180, 183, 188–191
    freedom from, 31, 173
    results of, 87, 238
    types of, 50–51, 71, 238

social sin, **71**, 238, **245**
Solomon, King, 76–77
soul, **69**, **245**
Stepanek, Mattie, 123
stewardship, 201, **245**
suffering, 8, 11, 28, 31
suicide, **156**, **245**
Sunday, 113, 139, 173
symbols, 224, 226

Talbot, Matt, Venerable, 194
teacher, 135–139
temple, 76, 156
Ten Commandments, **245**
    eighth, 164–165
    fifth, 155–156
    first, 111
    fourth, sixth and ninth, 147–149
    giving of, **60**–61
    Great Commandment and, 102–103
    meaning of, 234
    obedience to, 85, 225
    second, 112
    seventh and tenth, 200–201
    theft, 200
    third, 113
Teresa Benedicta, Saint, 74
theological virtues, 238
Thomas More, Saint, 162–163
Torah, 224
Tradition, 45, 224
Triduum, 28–31, **175**, 231, **245**
truth, 161–165

understanding, 39, 214, 237
unity, 147, 209

Venerable, 229
Veneration of the Cross, 231
venial sin, **70**, 183, 238, **245**
virtue, **238**
vocation, 120–**121**, 122–123, **245**
vows, 148–**149**, **245**

Way of the Cross, 28
widow's contribution, 201
wisdom, 39, 214, 224, 227, 237
Wisdom books, 222, 224
wonder and awe (fear of the Lord), 39, 215,
    237
worship, **111**, **245**

Yi Sung-hun, Saint, 220

Zacchaeus, 180, 188–189

## Illustration Credits

8-9 Frank Ordaz; 12-13 Maurie Manning; 16-17 Simone Boni; 20-21 Dan Brown; 28-29 Joel Spector; 32 Nick Harris; 36 Dennis Lyall. 42 (bkgd) Stacey Schuett; 44 (bl) James M. Effler; 45 (br) Judy Stead; 48 (bl) Lois Woolley; 45 (b) Dan Brown; 52 (bl) Michael Jaroszko; 53 (tr) Michael Jaroszko; 53 (br) Judy Stead; 56 (bl) Lois Woolley; 57 (b) Ezra Tucker; 58 (bl) Tom Newsom; 59 (cr) Mark Stevens; 60 (bl) Corey Wolfe; 61 (br) Judy Stead; 64 Lois Woolley. 71 (br) Judy Stead; 74 Lois Woolley; 76 (bl) Cathy Diefendorf; 81 (br) Judy Stead; 82 Lois Woolley; 84 (bl) Jeff Preston; 84 (br) Jeff Preston; 86 (bl) Jeff Spackman; 89 (br) Judy Stead; 90 (bl) Lois Woolley. 94 (b) Peter Church; 96 (br) Steve Adler; 100 (cr) Judy Stead; 100 (bl) Lois Woolley; 102 (bl) Roger Payne; 104 (bl) Karen Patkau; 107 (b) Judy Stead; 108 Lois Woolley; 110 (b) Adam Hook; 113 (br) Judy Stead; 116 (bl) Lois Woolley. 119 (br) Yvonne Gilbert; 120 (b) Mike Jaroszko; 121 (bl) Judy Stead; 126 (bl) Lois Woolley; 128 (bl) Philip Howe; 129 (cr) Philip Howe; 134 (cr) Judy Stead; 134 (bl) Lois Woolley; 136 (b) Dominick D'Andrea; 137 (cr) Dominick D'Andrea; 141 (br) Judy Stead; 142 (bl) Lois Woolley. 147 (tr) Philip Howe; 152 (bl) Lois Woolley; 155 (tr) Robert Sauber; 160 (bl) Lois Woolley; 162 (b) Jeff Preston; 168 (bl) Lois Woolley. 178 (bl) Lois Woolley; 179 (br) Philip Howe; 180 (b) Jeff Preston; 182 (b) Yuan Lee; 186 (bl) Lois Woolley; 188 (b) Doug Fryer; 191 (br) Adam Hook; 194 (bl) Lois Woolley. 198 (bl) Peter Church; 201 (cr) Kevin Torline; 204 (bl) Lois Woolley; 208 (b) Dean Kennedy; 212 (bl) Lois Woolley; 214 (bkgd) Kevin Torline; 220 (bl) Lois Woolley.

## Photo Credits

1 (l) Rubberball Productions; 1 (r) Comstock Images; 2 Richard Hutchings/Photo Edit; 6 PHOTOMONDO/Getty Images; 10-11 Hutchings Photography; 10 (bkgd) PhotoAlto/Creatas; 11 Hutchings Photography; 14-15 Don Farrall/Getty Images; 15 Ariel Skelley/Corbis; 18-19 Benelux Press/Index Stock; 22-23 zefa/Masterfile; 23 Richard Hutchings; 24-25 Richard Hutchings/Photo Edit; 26-27 David Greenwood/Getty Images; 27 (i) PhotoDisc; 30-31 (b) Daryl Benson/Masterfile; 30-31 (t) Corel; 31 Richard Hutchings; 34-35 Rich Reid/Getty Images; 35 PhotoDisc; 38-39 Corel; 39 (b) Richard Hutchings; 39 (t) PhotoDisc. 41 (bl) Eric Camden; 41 (bkgd) Adam Peiperl/CORBIS; 41 (bkgd) Adam Peiperl/CORBIS; 41 (bkgd) Adam Peiperl/CORBIS; 45 (cr) Thinkstock/Royalty-Free/Getty Images; 46 (br) Tom McCarthy/Photo Edit; 49 (b) Brian Minnich; 50 (cl) Jacqui Hurst/CORBIS; 51 (br) Sonny Senser; 51 Jewish Museum/Art Resource, NY ; 54 (cr) Bill Wittman; 59 (bl) Sonny Senser; 61 (bkgd) Royalty-Free/CORBIS; 64 (cr) Ed McDonald. 67 (b) Eric Camden; 67 (bc) Royalty-Free/CORBIS; 68 (br) Bettmann/CORBIS; 69 (cr) Ariel Skelley/CORBIS; 69 (bl) Jim Whitmer; 70 (bl) LWA-Dann Tardif/CORBIS; 71 (c) James W. Porter/CORBIS; 72 (br) Paul Vozdic/The Image Bank/Getty Images; 74 (cr) Jack Holtel/Photographik Company; 75 (b) Ed McDonald; 77 (cr) Cleve Bryant/PhotoEdit; 77 (br) Jim Whitmer; 78 (bl) Portland Art Museum/Gift of the Samuel H. Kress Foundation; 79 (cr) Richard Hutchings/PhotoEdit; 80 (br) Tom & Dee Ann McCarthy/CORBIS; 83 (cl) Royalty-Free/Getty Images; 83 (bl) Royalty-Free/Corbis; 83 (bkgd) Royalty-Free/Creatas; 83 (cl) Royalty-Free/Corbis; 85 (tr) Harcourt 85 (bl) David Young-Wolff/Photo Edit; 87 (bl) Sonny Senser; 88 (br) Jeff Grenberg/PhotoEdit; 90 (cr) Brian Leng/Corbis. 93 (bl) Ed McDonald; 95 (br) Sonny Senser; 97 (bkgd) Ed McDonald; 98 (br) Photodisc Blue/Royalty-Free/Getty Images; 101 (b) Brian Minnich; 101 (br) Brian Minnich; 101 (bc) Brian Minnich; 101 (bkgd) Ed McDonald; 103 (c) Kwame Zikomo/SuperStock; 103 (cr) Skjold Photographs; 105 (cr) Roger Ball/Corbis Stock Market; 106 (right) Gene Plaisted/The Crosiers; 109 (bl) Ed McDonald; 111 (br) Jim Whitmer; 111 (cr) Bill Wittman; 112 (bl) Myrleen Ferguson Cate/PhotoEdit; 113 (cr) Paul Barton/CORBIS; 114 (br) Eric Camden; 116 (cr) Ed McDonald. 121 (tr) Gene Plaisted/The Crosiers; 122 (bl) Jim Whitmer ; 123 (cr) Mattie Stepanek; 124 (br) Eric Camden; 126 (cr) Jack Holtel/Photographik Company; 127 (cl) Culver Pictures, Inc/Superstock; 127 (bl) David Turnley/CORBIS; 127 (br) Culver Picture, Inc/Superstock; 130 (bl) Giambologna/Arte & Immagini srl/CORBIS; 131 (cr) Gene Plastaid/The Crosiers; 132 (cr) Gene Plastaid/The Crosiers; 132 (cr) Gene Plastaid/The Crosiers; 132 (cr) Gene Plastaid/The Crosiers; 132 (cr) Gene Plastaid/The Crosiers; 132 (cr) Gene Plastaid/The Crosiers; 135 (b) Eric Camden; 137 (bl) Jim Whitmer; 138 (b) AFP/CORBIS; 139 (cr) Gene Plastaid/The Crosiers; 140 (cr) Juan de Juanes/Superstock; 142 (cr) Brooklyn Productions/The Image Bank/Getty Images. 145 (b) Ariel Skelley/Corbis; 145 (bkgd) Patrick Johns/Corbis ; 146 (bl) Eric Camden; 147 (bl) Jim Whitmer; 148 (bl) Ken Reid/Taxi/Getty Images; 149 (tr) JOEL SARTORE/National Geographic/Getty Images; 150 (br) Frank Siteman/Photo Edit; 152 (cr) Roy Morsch/Corbis; 153 (b) Ed McDonald; 154 (cl) Bettman/CORBIS; 154 (bl) Pierre Perrin/CORBIS SYGMA; 154 (bl) David Tumley/CORBIS; 154 (br) Bettman/CORBIS; 155 (cr) ROYALTY-FREE/Getty Images; 156 (bl) Stephen Simpson/Taxi/Getty Images; 157 (cr) Jim Whitmer Stock; 158 Florian Franke/SuperStock; 158 (br) Andy Sacks/Stone/Getty Images; 161 (b) Eric Camden; 163 (cl) Bettmann/CORBIS; 163 (cr) Bettmann/CORBIS; 164 (bl) Jose Luis Pelaez, Inc/CORBIS; 164 (bc) Photodisc Green/Royalty-Free/Getty Images; 165 (tr) Tony Freeman/Photo Edit; 166 (br) Rubberball Productions/Royalty-free/Getty Images; 167 (br) Tom & Dee Ann McCarthy/Corbis; 168 (cr) Ariel Skelley/CORBIS. 171 (c) Frank Cezus/Taxi/Getty Images; 171 (cr) Frank Cezus/Taxi/Getty Images; 171 (bl) Eric Camden; 171 (bc) Frank Cezus/Taxi/Getty Images; 171 (br) Frank Cezus/Taxi/Getty Images; 171 (bkgd) Royalty-Free/Corbis; 172 (cr) Michael Keller/CORBIS; 172 (cr) Tobi Corney/Stone/Getty Images; 172 (bc) Pascal Crapet/Stone/Getty Images; 172 (br) Sonny Senser; 175 (cr) Gene Plastaid/The Crosiers; 176 (br) Eric Camden; 178 (cr) Sonny Senser; 181 (cl) Elio Ciol/Corbis Rights Managed; 181 (c) Ed McDonald; 181 (cr) Royalty-Free/Corbis ; 181 (cr) Royalty-Free/Corbis; 181 (bl) Jim Whitmer; 183 (cr) Myrleen Ferguson Cate/PhotoEdit; 184 (br) Bill Wittman; 186 (cr) Ed McDonald; 187 (b) Ed McDonald; 189 (br) Jim Whitmer; 190 (bl) Gene Plastaid/The Crosiers; 192 (br) Tony Freeman / Photo Edit. 197 (br) Brian Minnich; 199 (tr) George Disario/CORBIS; 199 (bl) Jim Whitmer; 200 (bl) Victoria Bowen; 202 (br) David Young-Wolff/Photo Edit; 205 (b) Brian Minnich; 206 (cl) Maryknoll Bolivia Photos; 206 (bl) Maryknoll Ministry; 207 (tr) Maryknoll Ministry; 207 (cr) Maryknoll Ministries; 207 (bl) Jim Whitmer Stock; 210 (b) Sonny Senser; 212 (cr) Joe Carlson/Corbis; 213 (b) Ed McDonald; 213 (bkgd) Ed McDonald; 215 (br) Jim Whitmer; 216 (tr) Royalty-Free/Corbis; 216 (br) Michael Newman/PhotoEdit, Inc.; 217 (tl) Royalty-Free/CORBIS; 217 (bl) Ed Kashi/CORBIS; 217 (bkgd) Ed McDonald; 218 (cr) Royalty-Free/CORBIS; 222-223 Richard Hutchings; 223 (t) Myrleen Ferguson Cate/Photo Edit; 224 Ingram Publishing; 225 Richard Hutchings; 226 Father Gene Plaisted, OSC; 228 Pizzoli Alberto/Corbis Sygma; 230 (l) Father Gene Plaisted, OSC; 230 (r) Photos.com; 231 Corel; 234 Clipart.com; 235 Royalty-Free/Corbis; 236 Photodisc; 240 Thinkstock/Getty Images.

## Acknowledgements

For permission to reprint copyrighted material, grateful acknowledgment is made to the following sources:

*Hinshaw Music, Inc.:* Lyrics from "Go Now in Peace" by Natalie Sleeth. Lyrics © 1976 by Hinshaw Music, Inc.

*Hope Publishing Co., Carol Stream, IL 60188:* Lyrics from "Jesu, Jesu" by Tom Colvin. Lyrics © 1969 by Hope Publishing Co. Lyrics from "Shout for Joy" by David Mowbray. Lyrics © 1982 by Jubilate Hymns, Ltd.

*Hyperion:* From "Peace of Patience" in *Journey Through Heartsongs* by Mattie Stepanek. Text copyright © 2001 by Mattie Stepanek.

*International Commission on English in the Liturgy:* From the English translation of "Psalm 117: Go Out to All the World" in *Lectionary for Mass.* Translation © 1969, 1997 by International Committee on English in the Liturgy, Inc.

*Jack Prelutsky:* From "Me I Am!" in *The Random House Book of Poetry for Children* by Jack Prelutsky. Text copyright © by Jack Prelutsky.

*Patricia Joyce Shelly:* Lyrics from "All Grownups, All Children" by Patricia Joyce Shelly. Lyrics © 1977 by Patricia Joyce Shelly.

*Viking Penguin, a division of Penguin Group (USA) Inc.:* "The Creation" from *God's Trombones* by James Weldon Johnson. Text copyright 1927 by the Viking Press, Inc.; text copyright renewed © 1955 by Grace Nail Johnson.